P9-ELV-872

A Beginner's Guide to Investing

How to Grow Your Money the Smart and Easy Way

by Alex H. Frey

IvyBytes

IvyBytes

www.ivybytes.com

TABLE OF CONTENTS

Preface

Introduction

Chapter 1 - How to Double Your Money Every Seven Years: The Parable of Jill and Average Joe

Chapter 2 - Laying A Solid Foundation: How to Make Sense of the Investment World

Chapter 3 -How to Get Off to the Right Start: A Practical Guide to Choosing an Investment Account

Chapter 4 - How to Save Tens of Thousands of Dollars in Taxes, Without Opening an Offshore Bank Account (or Doing Anything Unethical)

Chapter 5 - Getting Organized: How to Form Your Own Personal Investing Plan

Chapter 6 - Why You Need to Know Your Investing Alphas and Betas: A Guide To Investment Returns

Chapter 7 - Moving Beyond the Stock Market: An Introduction to Asset Classes

Chapter 8 - Why the S&P 500 Is Not Good Enough: How to Use the Principles of Diversification to Choose an Intelligent Asset Allocation

Chapter 9 - Putting It Into Practice: How to Painlessly Implement Your Target Asset Allocation Using ETFs

Chapter 10 - Making It Bulletproof: How to Manage for the Long-Term with a Lockbox (and a Sandbox)

PREFACE

Investing is a topic that can be as broad, as deep, and as complicated as you want it to be. And at various times in my investing career, I have reveled in those complexities, whether it was figuring out how to measure the risk of a portfolio of credit-default swaps, or assessing the impact of rising meat consumption in China on an Australian chemicals company.

But somewhat paradoxically, investing is also a field that can be as simple as you want it to be. There are less than a handful of principles that, if mastered, get you 95+% of the way to an optimal portfolio: stay diversified, keep expenses low, have a plan, save and invest early and often. If you can internalize these principles, it is certainly possible to spend as little as four or five hours a year on your investments.

But here's the real rub: That simple approach often outperforms the more complicated approach. The vast majority of individual investors actually actively harm themselves trying to pick investments that they think are going to make them rich, when a more passive but rational strategy that adhered to the core principles would perform much better. Investing is one field where, once you learn the basics, a little bit of laziness can actually be rewarded.

The goal of this book is to show you how simple investing can be, and to give you enough of a peek of some more advanced topics that you can go on later to make it as simple or complicated as you desire.

Alex Frey
alex@ivybytes.com
March 2013

INTRODUCTION

This short introduction will go over some important features of this book, including how you can use it most effectively and how it was made.

HOW TO GET THE MOST VALUE OUT OF THIS BOOK

The Ivy Bytes series of books is designed to get you up to speed on a topic faster than anything else on the market.

- Every chapter begins with an overview of the material to be discussed.
- If you want to dive further into a topic, there is a further reading section at the end of each chapter that contains suggestions. **For readers of the paper version of this book, all suggested links have been condensed into one document that is freely available at *www.ivyvest.com/book-resources.***
- Especially important information **is presented in boldface to draw your attention to it**.
- The Further Reading section at the end of each chapter contains a list of the very best outside material on a subject, and is a great starting point for digging further. Where possible, these lists include clickable links to the material.

HOW THIS GUIDE WAS MADE

The process for creating Ivy Bytes guides is simple:

1. The guides' authors have an extensive background in their subject. Then they dig through countless newspaper and journal articles to get even more up to date on the latest thinking.

2. They analyze this trove of information and pick out the most pertinent, important, and well-supported pieces—the material that everyone fluent in a topic should understand.

3. They synthesize this material into an appropriate length of easily digestible content and include links to the "best of the rest."

A Note About the Products Included in This Book

Investing is a subject that has an extremely practical and actionable aspect to it, unlike, say, the history of 13th century France (which also might be very interesting, but is generally not something most people need to practice in their actual lives). This book was written to be as practical and actionable as possible, and in several places it made sense to mention the names and even ticker symbols of products that could be used to follow the strategies discussed.

Neither the author, nor the publisher, nor anyone involved in this book has a financial stake in any financial product mentioned in the book. Nor does anyone receive any kind of compensation from any of the products or companies mentioned. Many of the suggested products are from Vanguard, which is a customer-owned financial institution similar to a credit union.

NEW – Accompanying Website

Thanks to the success of this book, there is now an accompanying website that features additional information on investing, free tutorials on asset allocation, behavioral investing, portfolio management, risk, and the financial industry, and a subscription service that will suggest a low cost, tax efficient, optimally diversified ETF portfolio and send you an alert when you need to rebalance or make a move. Links will be included where appropriate. www.ivyvest.com

CHAPTER 1

HOW TO DOUBLE YOUR MONEY EVERY SEVEN YEARS:

THE PARABLE OF JILL AND AVERAGE JOE

OVERVIEW

A small initial investment can increase to a surprisingly large amount if it is held over several decades thanks to an amazing property of returns known as "compound interest." Most investors fail to realize this potential for vast wealth creation both because they start saving too late in their career and because they fail to achieve even an average rate of return due to fees and investment mistakes. The epidemic of financial illiteracy that underlies both of these mistakes can cost the average investor more than $500,000 over the course of a lifetime.

THE PARABLE OF JILL AND AVERAGE JOE

Jill and "Average Joe" are similar in many aspects:

- Each goes to a four-year college and graduates at age 22.

- Each enters the workforce making $40,000 a year.

- Each retires at 65 and lives the next 20 years off of accumulated savings.

- Each goes through the typical ups and downs that impact finances—things like unexpected job loss, marriage, and having one more kid than the "five year plan" called for.

Through it all, Jill and Average Joe both manage to make saving money a priority. Over the long-term each manages to put an average of 10% of total income into a retirement fund, only taking a break for three years in their mid-30s when family expenses and job concerns made saving too much of a sacrifice.

In fact, Jill and Average Joe differ in only two regards:

1. Jill starts saving immediately upon entering the workforce at age 22. Average Joe waits until he is 30 to begin saving, reasoning that retirement is still so far off.

2. Jill buys an index mutual fund that tracks the overall stock market, never touching her money and earning the same return as the overall stock market. Average Joe "tinkers" with his portfolio, purchasing some mutual funds through his financial advisor and investing in stocks whenever he gets a particularly juicy tip from his neighbor. Joe earns the same return as the average investor in the stock market.

When they retire at age 65, Jill and Average Joe both check the balance on their investment accounts to see what kind of lifestyle the next 20 years will bring. **Jill finds she has accumulated $967,000. Average Joe's portfolio has grown to less than 1/3 of this amount: $309,000**[1] (both figures have been adjusted for inflation).

The difference does not stop there. Provided their investment habits continue into retirement, **Jill will be able to earn as much as $84,000 a year from her** investments.[2] Average Joe **will spend his retirement living from Social Security check to Social Security check, receiving only $15,000 a year from his investments.**

The rest of this chapter will explore why such a huge difference exists between two people with such strikingly similar earning and saving habits, and where Average Joe went so horribly wrong. Because at its core, the parable of Jill and Average Joe represents the difference between the kind of investment returns millions of Americans *should be* earning, versus the kind that they actually *are* earning.

THE MIRACLE OF COMPOUND INTEREST

A Beginner's Guide to Investing

There are two things you can do with money: use it to purchase goods or services, or save it. Since spending money is obviously more fun than saving it, one reason you might rationally choose to save anyway is the hope that, in doing so, you will be able to consume an even larger amount of goods or services at a later date.

Over the past century, those that have elected to invest their savings in the stock market have accomplished this goal. Money invested in the stock market has grown over long periods by an average of 10% a year. After accounting for the increase in the price of goods over time (inflation), the rate of growth is still an impressive 6% annual rate.[3] Of course, there has been considerable variation in returns from year to year and even decade to decade, but over the long term, savers have been rewarded.

An important feature of investment returns is something called *compound interest*. This means that it is not only the initial investment that appreciates in value, but also the gains on that initial investment. For example, we might expect that an investment of $100 that appreciates at the 10% annual rate of the stock market over the past century would appreciate to $110 after one year and $120 after two years. But if no money is taken out, then in the second year it is not only the initial investment ($100) that grows at 10%, but also the *gains* on the initial investment from the first year ($10). So after two years the investment is actually worth $121. After many years, the "gains on the gains" of an investment can become remarkably significant, as they result in what is called *exponential growth*, meaning that the dollar value of an investment increases at a faster and faster rate over time. This sharply rising curve is clear in Figure 1.

FIGURE 1 - THE VALUE OF A $1,000 INVESTMENT RETURNING 8% A YEAR

Although compound interest can seem pretty straightforward and simple to understand, its dramatic and counterintuitive implications can be surprising to even those that grasp the concept at a basic level. The *rule of 72* is a handy mathematical shortcut that illustrates the power of exponential growth over time.

> **Rule of 72: To determine the approximate number of years an investment will take to double in value, divide 72 by the average annual rate of return earned on the investment.**

So an investment with a 10% annual rate of return will double approximately every 7 years (72 divided by 10 is about 7).

What is really interesting is the effect that compound interest has when the holding period is extended beyond those 7 years. An investment that doubles every 7 years will double twice every 14 years (2 x 2), resulting in a quadrupling in value. Over 21 years it will increase 8 times (2 x 2 x 2); over 28 years it will increase 16 times (2 x 2 x 2 x 2); and over 35 years it will increase 32 times (2 x 2 x 2 x 2 x 2). Over 42 years—well within the holding period of a typical worker who starts saving early in life—it will increase an astonishing 64 times in value (2 x 2 x 2 x 2 x 2 x 2). This is why even a small amount of money, if allowed to accumulate over a long enough time period, can grow to an extraordinary fortune. Getting back to the parable, by starting her saving 10 years earlier than Average Joe, Jill was able to increase the time that compound interest could work for her, greatly increasing her retirement wealth.

Figure 2 shows the actual growth of $1 invested in the stock market in 1960. Although the ride is much bumpier than in our hypothetical example above, a worker that invested $1 of income in 1960 would have more than $100 today—about a 10% compound annual return (Of course, there is no guarantee that U.S. stocks will repeat this performance over the next 50 years).

FIGURE 2 - THE RETURN FROM $1 INVESTED IN THE U.S. STOCK MARKET IN 1960 (USING THE S&P 500 INDEX)

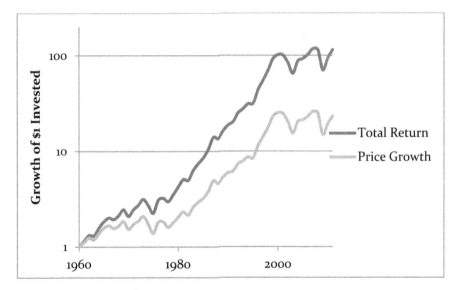

WHY MOST INVESTORS FAIL TO ACHIEVE THIS IDEAL

Seeing the miracle of compound interest propel Jill, with a very middle-class wage and modest savings level, to millionaire status by the time of her retirement, we might wonder why so many retirees are struggling. This question brings us to the second reason Jill is sipping piña coladas on a beach while Average Joe lives from Social Security check to Social Security check. The dirty little secret of the investing world is that even diligent savers like Average Joe largely fail to realize the ideal of returns that compound at the rate of the overall stock market.

Although a portfolio invested in the broad stock market would have increased at a 10% average rate over the last century, the average equity, or stock, investor has seen returns that significantly lag this rate. Over the past 20 years, data from DALBAR, a financial research company, indicate that **the average equity investor's return was about 4%, more than 5% below the return of the overall stock market.**[4] That's less than half!

There are two reasons why the returns of the average investor fall far short of the market:

1. **Fees. Whereas Jill paid relatively few fees, some 2% of Average Joe's assets disappeared into the hands of a financial advisor, investment manager, broker, or some combination thereof every year.**[v] Without these fees, Average Joe's portfolio would have been worth $432,000 instead of $309,000 at retirement, even with his late start.

2. **Poor investment decisions.** Historically, investors have been carried away by optimism when times are good and by pessimism when times are bad. The result is herd behavior, with money moving into stocks just in time to capture a market crash, and money moving out just in time to miss the start of a bull market. For instance, in 2000, investors added $325 billion to equity mutual funds, or *bought* into the market, at a time when the *S&P 500* (an index that serves as a benchmark indicator of the overall U.S. stock market condition) was high, with an index level in the range of 1400 to 1500. In 2002, investors *sold* a net of $12 billion when the S&P 500 was low, in the range of 820 to 1170.[6] **If he had made fewer investment mistakes, Average Joe's portfolio would have been**

worth $623,000 at the time of his retirement, even with his late start.

Each of these factors can really be attributed to one thing: financial illiteracy. Simply put, the average investor lacks the confidence to manage money on his or her own and lacks the ability to achieve even market-level returns. To put the cost of financial illiteracy into perspective, think of the result of the parable above. Jill and Average Joe were both alike except that Jill took the time to become financially literate at a young age, and Joe did not, pushing off savings until he was at a stage where he could hire an advisor. **To Average Joe, financial illiteracy seemed to "cost" only 2% a year—far less than he was making on his investments. But over the course of his lifetime, his ignorance would cost him some $500,000 in lost wealth.** Figure 3 concludes this chapter by looking at the dramatic effect that financial illiteracy can have on a retirement portfolio.

FIGURE 3 — JOE'S REFUSAL TO SAVE DURING HIS 20S AND INVESTMENT MISTAKES THROUGHOUT HIS LIFE LEFT HIM WITH ABOUT 1/3 OF THE RETIREMENT WEALTH OF AVERAGE JILL, DESPITE THEIR SIMILARITIES

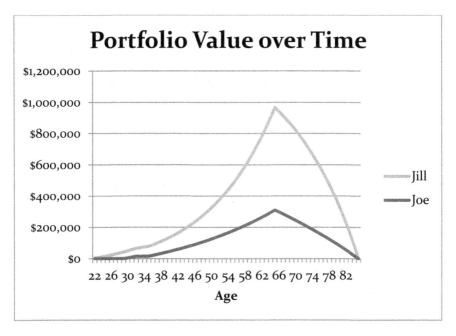

A Note About the Return Figures Used in This Book

In several places in this book, examples with numbers are provided to illustrate a point. These numbers should not be taken literally. Where possible, I have based them on real historical data – for instance the stock market really has returned an average of 10% a year over the last 150 years. Nobody can argue with that – it is simply a fact.

However, for the sake of illustrating the relevant point and not getting bogged down in complexity, I often assume that a return is constant, when, as you can see in Figure 2, returns can vary greatly from year to year and even decade to decade, and nothing is certain in the stock market. An example showing a constant 8% return that is used to show the power of a tax-free account should not, for instance, be taken to mean that you can get constant 8% returns anywhere – you clearly cannot in 2013.

Similarly, the point of this chapter is not to argue that you should be able to double your money every seven years like clockwork, but to point out that because of the amazing properties of compound interest, a seemingly small annual return can really add up over time. The crux of this chapter is true whether returns average 4%, 6%, 8% or 20% in the future – I chose 10% because it is the data-point that we actually have from history.

Further Reading

- *Predictably Irrational,* by Dan Ariely, talks about the psychology behind many of our poor investment decisions in a manner that is friendly for the layperson.

- *Stocks for the Long Run* by Jeremy Siegel and *Triumph of the Optimists* by Elroy Dimson both discuss historical stock market returns in detail.

CHAPTER 2

LAYING A SOLID FOUNDATION:

HOW TO MAKE SENSE OF THE INVESTMENT WORLD

OVERVIEW

At its most basic level, an investment represents an exchange between two parties—one who needs money now in order to build something that will generate money in later years, and another who has money now but would like to postpone using it until the future. Stocks and bonds represent two different ways of structuring this kind of across-time agreement. Secondary markets like the New York Stock Exchange allow investors to "trade" their initial investments to others in exchange for cash. The intrinsic value of any investment is just the future income stream that it will produce, discounted back to the present to account for the time value of money.

WHAT AN INVESTMENT REALLY IS

In a modern world complete with a litany of complicated investment options, it is easy to lose sight of what an investment in the financial markets actually represents. It can be instructive to imagine what things would have been like in a simpler time and place—an ancient town where "Ted" and "Bill" are two farmers and neighbors.

In our scenario, Ted's farm is in the land of plenty. He has had several good farming years and has more food stockpiled than his family will be able to eat. He would like to be able to exchange food today for food in the future, when he might not be as lucky in his harvest, or as able to work.

Bill is just starting out, and would like to spend time working on enlarging the farm and building a new barn so that he can expand his operation in future years in order to be more like Ted. However, if he spends his time enlarging the farm he will not be able to harvest his crops this year. This would not make Bill's hungry wife and kids very happy.

Since Bill needs to obtain extra food now in order to produce more food later, and Ted has extra food now and would like to get more food later, it seems that a mutually beneficial trade should be possible. But the problems in structuring this trade are significant, since it is taking place across time. Ted wants to be sure that he will get as much or more food in the future as he is giving up now. Otherwise he could grind or dry his corn, put it into storage, and lock it away from Bill's hungry children. Ted also naturally worries that Bill will just run off with the extra food and never deliver on his end of the deal. Finally, Ted wonders whether there are other farmers like Bill, in towns far away, who might give him a better deal.

For all their complexity, the modern financial markets evolved to solve precisely these kinds of age-old problems. In the next section, we will look at how stocks and bonds represent two different ways that Bill and Ted could have structured a mutually beneficial agreement.

EXPLAINING STOCKS AND BONDS

The first way that Ted and Bill might have decided to structure their arrangement is a simple "pay you back later" agreement, equivalent to saying "Can I borrow your car? I promise I will bring it back in two hours." To make the deal attractive for Ted, Bill might offer to give him an additional three bushels of corn at the end of every year until the debt has been paid off ("Can I borrow your car? I'll fill it up with gas before I bring it back"). So Ted would receive yearly corn payments in addition to the return of his initial investment at the end of the loan term.

If Ted and Bill had structured the arrangement in this way, they would have created something similar to a bond. Today, **bonds are a type of debt that represents an IOU from a user of money (the "debtor") such as a company or government, to a provider of money (the "creditor") such as an investor**. In exchange for immediate use of the creditor's money, the debtor agrees to make a periodic interest payment, as well as to return the full amount owed at the end of a fixed term. Creditors can make a positive return over the course of the investment because they get their initial investment back at the end of the term, and they receive interest payments in the mean time. For our example of Bill and Ted, let's say the term is three years. Table 1 shows the two farmers' actions over that time.

TABLE 1 – TED AND BILL'S EXCHANGES UNDER A "BOND" ARRANGEMENT

Yr	Ted action	Bill action
1	Pay 100 bushels to Bill.	Receive 100 bushels from Ted. Use to build larger farm.
2	Receive interest of 5 bushels from Bill.	Pay interest of 5 bushels to Ted. Continue farm improvements.
3	Receive 105 bushels of corn from Bill.	Pay back loan (100 bushels) and interest (5 bushels) to Ted.

Ted and Bill could have also structured their arrangement another way. Ted could provide Bill with 100 bushels of corn in exchange for a portion of the ownership of the new farm, say 10%. This way, Ted would be entitled to 10% of the future production of Bill's farm. If the improvements to the farm were successful, Ted could receive much more corn than he initially gave up, earning a positive return on his investment. If the improvements were unsuccessful, he might end up receiving less than he initially gave Bill. This kind of arrangement allows Ted and Bill to share in the risk of the project, and is similar to a stock. Table 2 shows each man's actions in a stock-like agreement, where Ted is investing in Bill's "company."

TABLE 2 - TED AND BILL'S ACTIONS UNDER A "STOCK" ARRANGEMENT

Year	Ted action	Bill action
1	Pay 100 bushels to Bill.	Receive 100 bushels from Ted. Use to build

			larger farm.
2		Receive dividend from Bill: 10% of corn production	Pay Ted 10% of corn production
3... and on		Receive corn dividend from Bill: 10% of corn production	Pay Ted 10% of corn production

There are a couple reasons Bill and Ted might prefer the "stock" arrangement to the "bond" arrangement. If the farm improvements Bill was planning were relatively risky—for instance, if he was building a new kind of production machinery and there was a chance it would not work as planned—he might prefer the stock arrangement since the payments he would have to make to Bill would vary with the success of the project, eliminating his personal risk of not being able to make a payment. For his part, Ted might also prefer the stock arrangement since it gives him the potential for a greater return if the project goes well. With the bond, Ted's upside was security—knowing that he would definitely get his money back (we will assume for now that Bill will not default on the loan) plus some small interest payments, but with the stock arrangement he has the potential of earning much more corn than he invested.

Today, **stocks are certificates issued by companies when they do not have the cash on hand to build a new factory, launch a new product, or otherwise invest in their business. In exchange for providing needed money, investors receive partial ownership of the company**. If the company makes profits in the future, it will give a portion of its earnings to its owners in annual or quarterly payments known as *dividends*. By purchasing a stock, an investor has the opportunity to make a positive return over the course of the investment if the total dividends received from the company are greater than the value of his or her initial investment (this is assuming the investment is held forever—we will get to secondary markets in a bit).

Thus far, we have assumed that the circumstances for Ted and Bill do not change between the time they enter into the agreement and the time the agreement is complete. But imagine that shortly after giving his surplus food to Bill, Ted's farm is overrun by corn-eating locusts. He could try to get his food back from his neighbor, but Bill has already held his fields fallow for a year, and there is not enough to feed both families. A solution to this problem could be for Ted to sell his contract with Bill to a third farmer, "Jane," who also has a surplus of corn. Jane would give Ted corn now in exchange for receiving future corn payments from Bill.

The modern equivalent of this kind of re-selling of contracts takes place in secondary markets like the New York Stock Exchange. **Secondary markets for financial contracts let an individual who initially invested in a stock or bond sell it to another individual that would like to take it over.** The prices for stocks and bonds that are frequently quoted in newspapers and on the Internet are simply the most recent price at which these secondary exchanges between individuals are taking place.

One downside of both stocks and bonds is that many individual investors do not have enough money or time to manage a very large portfolio of them. Mutual funds arose as a solution to this problem. **A *mutual fund* pools together money from many different investors and invests this larger pool in a portfolio of stocks.** Each investor in the mutual fund owns a portion of this portfolio and receives a portion of any income or investment gains. Mutual funds are managed by a professional investor who is usually employed by a company like Fidelity or T. Rowe Price.

WHERE THE "VALUE" OF AN INVESTMENT COMES FROM

Often, commentators will talk about a stock or bond as being particularly "overvalued" or "undervalued." Such a description poses the question of how to define "fair value."

The theory of *intrinsic value* says that an investment's price should equal the value it would have to a buyer who planned to hold it forever (even though, with the advent of secondary markets, most investors do not actually do so). Investors who plan to hold a stock or bond forever are not concerned about what the asset is trading for on secondary markets, they are simply concerned with the value that they will receive from the annual or semi-annual interest, or dividend payments. **Thus the *value of a stock* that is correctly priced today should be the present value of its future dividends.**

The idea that a string of dividends going forever into the future has a "present value" seems a bit strange at first. But it makes complete sense in the context of what economists call the *time value of money*. The basic idea is that receiving $1 today is worth more than receiving $1 five years from now. You can think about this in three different ways:

1. If you had a dollar today you could invest it in a guaranteed bank account or certificate of deposit (CD).

2. You can buy more things with a dollar today than you will be able to with a dollar five years from now. This is because of inflation, the slow rise in the cost of living over time. For instance, a dollar in 1970 bought four loaves of bread; today it will not even get you half a loaf.

3. If you are human, you probably would prefer to spend a dollar today, even if it *could* be used to buy the same things five years from now. Most of us prefer immediate gratification to delayed gratification. Given the choice of eating cake now or eating cake one week from now, we choose now. Which is not to mention that many of us have to spend money today for things like eating, which cannot be delayed indefinitely.

Because dividend payments received in the future are worth less than those received today, we need to apply a *discount rate* to them in order to express what they are worth to a rational investor today.

If we know or can observe what the time value of money is, than we can place a dollar value today on the promise of $1 five years from now. In doing so, we are "discounting it back to the present." And if we can place a current dollar value on the promise of $1 five years from now, then there is no reason we cannot place a current dollar value on any stream of future dividends or interest payments.

This is precisely what is needed to value a stock, bond, or any other kind of investment—estimate the income the investment will provide at each year in the future, and discount it back to the present at an appropriate time value of money.

A good estimate for the time value of money today is the interest rate on a very safe investment, such as U.S. Treasury bonds (IOUs from the U.S. government). There is a kind of Treasury bond known as a *zero-coupon bond*. If you purchase a zero-coupon bond, such as a U.S. savings bond, you receive a guaranteed amount of money at a specified time in the future, but you do not receive any interest payments until then. Because of this, the price of a zero-coupon bond that will pay us $1 ten years from now will be much less than $1 today, and this price is just the time value of money. For instance, if a ten year zero-coupon bond that pays $100 at maturity is selling for $60 today, then that means that $100 ten years from now is equivalent to 60 of today's dollars.

TABLE 3 — PRESENT VALUE CALCULATION FOR A HYPOTHETICAL INVESTMENT PAYING A $10 DIVIDEND FOR 5 YEARS

	Estimated dividend	Discount rate	Present value of dividends
Year 1	$10	1.1	$9.1
Year 2	$10	1.21	$8.3
Year 3	$10	1.33	$7.5
Year 4	$10	1.5	$6.8
Year 5	$10	1.61	$6.2
Value of investment (sum of present			$39.7

values)				

In the Bill and Ted example, the intrinsic value of Ted's investment will always be his best guess on how many bushels of corn Bill will give him in the future. This would vary with the probability of success of the project and/or Bill's credit worthiness. In today's markets, intrinsic value equates to the estimated future dividend or income stream of a company, discounted back to the present to reflect the time value of money and the riskiness of the investment.

WHY THE MARKETS MOVE AROUND SO MUCH MORE THAN YOU WOULD THINK

It may seem difficult to explain the wild gyrations of the stock market in the context of a theory that says stock prices should, in principle, never diverge from their intrinsic value. Large market volatility can be a result of three factors.

First, it is exceedingly difficult to estimate what the intrinsic value of a company is, since this rests on estimating profits forever into the future and discounting them back to current dollars at an equally uncertain time value of money. Estimates can change dramatically based on changes in technology, competition, the regulatory environment, geopolitics, the economy, estimates of future inflation, and the individual preference for money now vs. later. Since we live in a dynamic world where all of these are changing on a daily basis, rational estimates of intrinsic value are certain to change with time.

Second, the markets are composed of human participants and may not be immune to emotional factors such as fear and greed. Human emotions may have a particularly large role today because the average holding period of a stock has shrunk to only four months according to the *Economist*.[7] This short holding period creates an incentive for market participants to play what prominent economist John Maynard Keynes referred to as a "beauty contest."[8] This tendency is an especial temptation for professional fund managers and others who are judged by short-term measures such as the performance of their fund over the past quarter. The idea is that the markets can, in periods of intense speculation, come to resemble a game where the objective is not so much to figure out which companies are the most valuable, but instead to figure out which companies most investors will think are the most valuable. Rational investors may buy into shares trading at prices that are much higher than any reasonable estimate of their intrinsic value if they think that others will be willing in the future to purchase those shares at even higher prices still. This kind of dynamic can create market volatility independent of changes in the fundamentals of a business or the economy. Of course, perception can sometimes become reality...

On that note, the third important piece of the volatility puzzle may come from what billionaire hedge-fund speculator George Soros describes as *reflexivity*. **The idea is that movements in stock prices do not just reflect estimates of the future, but they can, in fact, directly *impact* the future.** A recent example of this phenomenon is the 2008 financial crisis. Falling prices on investments like stocks at first reflected lower intrinsic value of assets as a result of deteriorations in the real economy. But falling prices then *caused* even further deteriorations in the economy because households and businesses looked at the lower values of their stocks, bonds, and houses, realized they were not as wealthy as they once had thought, and cut spending. When everyone cut spending at once, the economy deteriorated further, causing even more pressure on investment prices. Reflexivity can create markets that are susceptible to wild jumps from one extreme to the other.

FURTHER READING

Remember to see www.ivyvest.com/book-resources to get links to every article, book, or site discussed in further reading sections.

- Investopedia.com has a nice tutorial on the time value of money for those confused by the explanation in this guide.

- For those interested in learning more about the intrinsic value concept, Professor of Finance at the Stern School of Business at New York University Aswath Damodaran has posted slides on the subject.

- *Investing in the Stock Market: A Primer*, another Ivy Bytes book, contains a lengthier discussion on the time value of money and stock valuation.

Chapter 3

How to Get Off to the Right Start:

A Practical Guide to Choosing an Investment Account

Overview

Opening an investment account is a crucial first step to saving wisely. Today, you have the option to invest through a discount brokerage account, a mutual fund account, a full-service brokerage account, or even a bank account. You should pay extremely close attention to fees when choosing an account, since seemingly small yearly charges can act as sharp brakes on the amazing effects of compound interest. Discount brokerages are an appropriate choice for many, since they combine low fees with the widest selection of investment options. It is relatively easy to select a discount brokerage firm since competition has lowered fees substantially.

Why Expenses Matter—A Lot

Cooking is something that I have a love-hate relationship with. Although I love being able to control exactly what goes into my body, having an unlimited array of culinary possibilities, and saving money by not eating at restaurants, I hate figuring out what combinations of food will taste good, burning rice for the third time in two weeks, and spending time in front of a stove with a potholder and not in front of a TV with a beer. Frequently the tension of this dilemma is resolved with a takeout order. I am perfectly okay with this, because it is still relatively affordable to outsource this part of my life for $10 a meal or so. But if local takeout places were charging $10,000 a meal, you can bet I would be in a cooking class in no time. No one would eat out at those kinds of prices.

Yet an equivalent price structure exists in the world of investment management, and rather than learning to cook, most people are instead opting to pay $400,000 for a hamburger that has been sitting out in the sun too long.

To see why, let's bring back Jill and Average Joe.

Imagine each makes an identical $100k investment that earns 8% a year before fees. Jill invests directly in a low cost index fund that charges a fee of 0.2% of assets. Average Joe invests in an average mutual fund through an average financial advisor. The mutual fund charges a management fee of 1.3% of assets (not all funds are as expensive, but 1.3% is about average for an actively managed fund), and his financial advisor charges a fee of 1% of assets for selecting the fund on his behalf.

To Joe, it seems like it is well worth it to pay roughly 2% of his assets a year for the convenience of professional management, especially when his investments are easily earning more than this every year. But in actuality he is reducing his returns by a stunning amount over time. After 30 years, Jill's account would have grown to $952,000 whereas Joe's account would have grown to only $528,000. Solely by paying 2% a year less in fees, Jill will be nearly twice as wealthy as Joe. The fees that Joe paid did not seem high relative to the returns he was making at the time, but over the course of 30 years they ended up "costing" him $424,000, or four times his initial investment.

How to Cook Your Own Stock Market Stew

The first step to figuring out the right place to open an account is to decide what kind of company to do business with. There are four general choices: full-service brokerages, mutual fund companies, discount brokerages, and banks.

Discount brokerages, where you "eat your own cooking," are a compelling choice for many. **Discount brokerage accounts are low-cost online accounts** offered by firms like E*TRADE, Charles Schwab, and Fidelity. **These accounts allow do-it-yourself investors to purchase a large**

variety of common stocks, mutual funds, and exchange-traded funds (ETFs), making them a great one-stop shop for financial products. There is often no annual fee for using a discount brokerage. Instead, discount brokerage providers make money by charging a small commission every time you buy or sell a stock or mutual fund. Most brokerages charge between $5 and $15 per trade. Discount brokerages are the lowest cost way for most investors to access a wide variety of investments.

A *mutual fund account* from a company like T. Rowe Price or Vanguard is the investing equivalent of a chain restaurant. Mutual fund accounts allow investors to purchase funds sold by their parent company, but they do not enable investors to directly purchase stocks. However, larger fund families like Fidelity and Vanguard will likely also offer discount brokerage accounts. Discount brokerage accounts from mutual fund companies may be a compelling value since they let you invest in stocks alongside their own funds.

Mutual funds appeal to those that seek the professional management capabilities of a mutual fund manager. However, they often come with higher fees that, as we have seen, can lead to dramatically lower returns over the long term. Mutual fund fees can vary enormously from one company to another (and from one fund to another at the same company). Some firms charge 1.3% of assets or more to manage your money; others even add a "load" fee that will cost you as much as 5% of your money up front just for the privilege of investing in their fund (this goes to compensate the advisor that sold you the fund). There is virtually never a good reason to pay a load fee. Well-run mutual funds from companies like Vanguard and T. Rowe Price have much lower fees and do not charge a load.

Full-service brokerage accounts from the likes of Morgan Stanley and Goldman Sachs are the financial equivalent of hiring a private chef. These accounts are like discount brokerages except they offer more personal services like wealth management and advice, and they generally charge more. They appeal to those that want an investment adviser. Be aware that the advisor may be tempted to recommend investments that pay him or her a high commission (the financial term for a kickback), rather than what is best for you. **To avoid this, look for an advisor that is regulated as a** *Registered Investment Advisor* **(RIA),** and charges you a well-disclosed fee based on the percentage of the funds that you invest with him or her. RIAs have a legal, fiduciary responsibility to look out for your best interests. Brokers do not, even though they confusingly may still call themselves "investment advisors."

Although generally not considered investment accounts, *bank checking, savings, CDs,* and *money market accounts* are the financial equivalent of a TV dinner. Like the humble plastic-wrapped dinner, bank accounts have their advantages. The return earned from them is free of any risk, and money invested is guaranteed by the government. Moreover, money can easily be withdrawn from the account at full value whenever it is needed, a feature that economists call *liquidity*. Nonetheless, the compound return you can get over a lifetime from a bank account pales in comparison to the wealth creation opportunities from investing in the stock market. Checking and savings accounts are great places to keep money that might be needed in the next couple of years, but higher return assets like stocks and mutual funds will, on average, offer the potential for much higher returns over the long term. TV dinners have their time and place, but you do not want to live on them.

How to Choose Where to Open Your Discount Brokerage Account

Luckily, finding a good discount brokerage is a lot easier than learning how to cook. Competition amongst online providers has pushed trade costs to all-time lows, leaving more money in the pockets of smart individual investors. Large players like TD Ameritrade, E*TRADE, Scottrade, and Fidelity all have compelling offers and are good places to start. A few factors to consider in choosing a provider:

- You should not have to pay more than $10 per trade.

- You should not have to pay any monthly maintenance fees, regardless of the level of commissions you generate.

- You should have free access to online tools, calculators, and stock quotes.

- The minimum account size should be below the level you plan to invest.

Once you have decided on an appropriate provider (and it is difficult to go wrong in choosing between the main players), opening an account is easy. You need to know your Social Security number and other personal information and have access to a funding source like a bank account. Usually, you electronically transfer money from a bank account to a brokerage account using your bank routing number and checking account number (both of which are on your checks). Once your account is open, you may need to wait a few days for everything to clear, and then you will be able to begin investing! The remainder of this book will focus on what to do with your new account.

FURTHER READING

- If you are looking for a discount brokerage, our IvyVest sister site has an article that discusses the pros and cons of seven different options as well as a free tutorial on the financial industry.

- The Securities and Exchange Commission (SEC) offers a fairly readable overview of the things to consider before hiring an investment adviser.

Chapter 4

How to Save Tens of Thousands of Dollars in Taxes, Without Opening an Offshore Bank Account (or Doing Anything Unethical)

Overview

In modern times, the government has used tax incentives as a means of encouraging citizens to save for retirement. It is essential for the individual investor to consider the role of taxes in devising an investment strategy, as taxes represent the largest investment expense. Therefore, tax-advantaged accounts like the 401(k) and IRA offer extremely compelling advantages, as well as some limitations. Taxable accounts incur greater expenses, but also offer more flexibility. Most people will be best served by opening one of all three account types.

The Government's Role in Retirement Planning

For thousands of years of history, the best retirement planning that was available to the middle class was to have a lot of kids. Kids could grow up, take over the family farm, and tend to their parents in their retirement years. Government did not have much of a role to play.

This changed following the Great Depression and WWII. The Great Depression brought the government into the retirement industry in the form of Social Security, a program that taxes people during their working years and pays out benefits to them during their retirement years. Government wage controls during WWII also encouraged private companies to compete for workers by offering pension plans instead of higher salaries, starting a tradition of employer-provided retirement plans.

In the late 20th century it became evident that neither Social Security nor private pension plans would be sufficient to pay for the retirement of the baby boomer generation. The government responded again by offering tax breaks that encouraged workers to save and invest for their own retirements. The combination of these forces produced the Individual Retirement Account (IRA), and the 401(k) employer-provided retirement account.

This chapter will look at how you can take advantage of the IRA, 401(k), and traditional (taxable) investment account to save for your retirement. This complicated amalgamation of different account types has made things more confusing for the individual investor, but it has also opened the door to enormous tax savings that you do not want to pass up.

Being smart about taxes is not about "gaming" the system, it's about getting your fair share of the tax incentives that are available to all of us. And no Cayman Island bank accounts are required.

TAXES ARE THE MOST SIGNIFICANT INVESTMENT EXPENSE YOU WILL PAY

Just as paying seemingly modest fees for money management every year can stunningly reduce your wealth over time, paying seemingly modest taxes every year can sharply impact your quality of life in retirement. Money that is not in a tax-sheltered retirement account (more on these below) is subject to four types of taxes:

- **Income taxes**. Interest earned from bonds is taxed at the ordinary income rate, which can be as high as 35% at the federal level.

- **Capital gains taxes**. If an investment is sold for a higher price than it was purchased for, the difference is termed a *capital gain* and is subject to tax. If the investment producing the gain was held for a year or longer, a special capital gains tax rate of (usually) 15% applies. If the investment was held for less than a year, it is taxed at the full ordinary income rate (up to 35%).

- **Dividend taxes**. Dividends received from stocks are taxed either at the ordinary income rate or at a qualified dividend rate, which may be lower (currently 15% for most taxpayers).

- **State and local taxes**. States usually do not differentiate between sources of income, so whatever you make from your investments will be taxed at the income rate (unless you are lucky enough to live in a tax-free state like Nevada, Texas, or Washington).

Be aware that tax rates have changed markedly in the past and are likely to increase in the future.

Together, these taxes act as a sharp brake on the amazing effects of compound interest, which we covered in Chapter 1. To see the huge potential impact that taxes can make, let's assume that you are in the 33% tax bracket and have $100,000 invested in a long-term bond that pays out 6% interest a year. If you re-invest your proceeds every year, this money will actually compound at 6% inside a tax-sheltered account, growing to $575,000 over the course of 30 years. Outside a 401(k) or other tax-sheltered account, this money will compound at a true after-tax rate of only 4% (since 1/3 of the income will go to the government every year), growing to only $324,000 (see Figure 5). Once again, seemingly minor annual savings add up to a gigantic, $250,000 difference in final wealth over time.

FIGURE 5 — TAX-ADVANTAGED ACCOUNTS CAN COMPOUND WEALTH AT A MUCH FASTER RATE THAN REGULAR ACCOUNTS

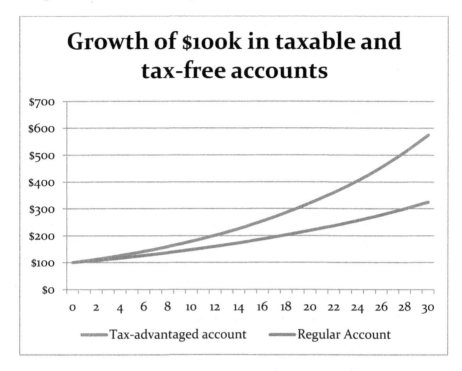

The two major tax-advantaged account types that you must become familiar with to be an informed investor are the 401(k) and the Individual Retirement Account (IRA).

THE 401(K): WORTH OPENING FOR THE MATCHING CONTRIBUTIONS AND KEEPING FOR THE TAX SAVINGS

A 401(k) is a retirement account that is provided by your employer. Employees can elect to have a portion of their wages deducted directly from their paycheck and invested in the 401(k). A 401(k) is often referred to as a direct contribution (DC) retirement plan, because employees bear all investment risk in the account. It is the contributions—not the benefits— that are guaranteed. With a more traditional defined-benefit (DB) pension plan, it is benefits that are guaranteed by the company (at least until they get into financial trouble like the auto companies and start negotiating everything...).

A Beginner's Guide to Investing

To see the advantages of a 401(k), we'll look at Janet, a 35-year-old middle manager making $50,000 a year. Investing in a 401(k) has three huge advantages for Janet:

1. **Janet's employer may automatically "match" a portion of her contribution, giving her free money.** Employers will often match a portion of employee contributions up to a certain level—this means that if you put in a given amount, your employer will make an automatic contribution on your behalf. Janet's company matches up to half of the first 6% of her salary that she contributes annually to her 401(k). This extra contribution can add up significantly over time. Janet's salary is $50,000 per year, so that means if she invests 6%, or $3000, in her 401(k), her employer will contribute another $1,500. After a 30-year period, this extra $1,500 a year will add $170,000 to the value of her retirement account if it is invested in a fund that earns an 8% average annual return . Automatic employer matches are essentially free money that employees would be foolish not to take advantage of.

2. **Janet can deduct her contribution from her income before calculating her taxes**. Let's use a simplified example to get an idea of the impact contributing to a tax-deferred account can have on income tax. Say Janet contributes $10,000 to her 401(k), then her taxable income will be reduced from $50,000 to $40,000. Janet is in a 25% tax bracket, so lowering her taxable income by $10,000 will save her as much as $2,500 dollars a year in taxes.

3. **Janet's investments will grow completely tax-free inside her 401(k) account.** Normally, interest on investments is taxed as income or dividends, but inside a 401(k) this money is allowed to grow tax-free until it is taken out. So Janet's investments inside her 401(k) will compound tax-free, as described above, and grow faster than if she had invested an equivalent amount of money outside the 401(k).

Although its huge benefits make it an important cornerstone of anyone's retirement plan, the 401(k) does come with three significant liabilities:

1. **Janet will face significant tax penalties if she needs to withdraw any money in her 401(k) before she turns 60.** This makes the 401(k) a poor place to save for short-term goals like a new car. However, if something totally unexpected does come up then Janet still has some options. For instance, she may be able to take a loan from the 401(k) and pay herself back with interest at a later date.

2. **Janet will be taxed on retirement withdrawals from her account at an ordinary income rate.** Although money inside a 401(k) compounds tax-free during the growth phase, the withdrawals made after age 60 are subject to income taxes. Depending on Janet's income in retirement, this could result in large taxes at that time. However, the huge benefits of compounding money at a tax-free rate make this a great tradeoff for most people.

3. **Janet's investment choices in a 401(k) will likely be limited to a set approved by her employer.** While some plans are quite good, this can severely limit the flexibility that Janet has in planning for her retirement. She might be forced to purchase a relatively high-cost and poor-performing mutual fund from a company that her employer has a relationship with. For this reason, many people choose to roll their 401(k) over into an IRA if they change jobs or retire.

THE IRA (INDIVIDUAL RETIREMENT ACCOUNT): A GREAT ALL-AROUND RETIREMENT SAVINGS VEHICLE

The IRA is a tax-advantaged account that was created by the government to encourage people to save for their retirement outside of employer provided plans. **A traditional IRA has the same tax advantages as a 401(k), but it is entirely self-managed, so it lacks the constraints in investment selection of the 401(k).**

The IRA does have two disadvantages relative to the 401(k):

1. **For many people, contributions are only fully tax deductible for those with an income below $56,000 (single filers).** For those who have an employer-sponsored retirement plan available to them, contributions to an IRA are deductible from taxable income only if you (the saver) have a net income of less than a limit defined by the IRS. For 2012 the limit for full deductibility is $58,000 for singles and $92,000 for couples filing a joint return ($169,000 if you file jointly and one of you is covered by a plan but the other is not). Higher income persons can still contribute and get the benefit of tax deferral on the income earned, but they cannot get a tax break on their contributions. This negates most of the advantage of the account. These limits do not apply if you do not have a 401(k) account available to you. If you are self-employed, you are eligible to start what is called a SEP IRA, and you may be able to contribute up to 25% of your profits or $50,000, whichever is lower.

2. **The contribution limit on a traditional IRA is significantly lower than on a 401(k).** In 2012, contributions to IRAs were limited to $5,000 a year for those under 50 and $6,000 dollars a year for those over 50. Compare that with $17,000 for the 401(k) for people of any age.

Those eligible for an IRA and a 401(k) can and should open both types of accounts.

ROTH OR TRADITIONAL? FLIP A COIN . . .

A further complication of IRA and (some) 401(k) accounts is that they actually come in two different varieties, *Roth* and *traditional*. Not all employers offer a Roth 401(k) (if yours does not, do not worry about it).

The basic difference between IRAs is that with a traditional account, contributions are pre-tax (or tax-deductible) and withdrawals are taxed at the income rate. With a Roth account, contributions are made after tax, but withdrawals are tax-free.

Much ink has been shed debating the relative merits of Roth and traditional accounts, but for most people, the differences in the two types of accounts are quite negligible compared to the huge benefits in fully using either one of them. In fact, **traditional and Roth accounts will produce a mathematically equivalent income in retirement for many people under many scenarios.** This is because the primary difference between the two accounts is one of timing—with a Roth account you pay taxes now but save money on taxes later, whereas with a traditional account you receive tax savings now but have to pay taxes later.

Here are some guidelines for deciding whether a Roth or traditional IRA is best for you:

- If you expect to be in a lower tax bracket in retirement than you are now, then a traditional account might be the best choice since it makes sense to take your tax deduction now, when it is worth more. This may be the case if you have only modest retirement savings and expect your retirement income to be much lower than your current income. If you expect to be in a higher tax bracket in retirement than you are now, then a Roth account might be for you. This may be the case if you have large retirement savings or if you receive a significant inheritance, for example.

- If you expect to be in a similar tax bracket but are worried that taxes will increase in the future in order to pay down large government deficits, a Roth account might be your best choice.

- If you are already "maxing out" the contributions to your retirement accounts and would like to be able to contribute more, then a Roth account might be your best choice. This is because you are contributing after-tax dollars to the Roth, so the effective contribution limit is greater.

- For IRA accounts, a Roth provides greater flexibility in the timing of withdrawals, which can be an important feature if you anticipate needing to access your funds prior to retirement or if you want to leave money to heirs. Roth accounts allow you to withdraw contributions (but not investment gains) at any time, they let you withdraw up to $10,000 for a first-time house at any time, and they let you refrain from ever taking withdrawals.

Table 4 summarizes the primary attributes of these most common types of retirement accounts:

TABLE 4 — KEY CHARACTERISTICS OF RETIREMENT ACCOUNTS

	TRADITIONAL 401(K)	ROTH 401(K)	TRADITIONAL IRA	ROTH IRA
AVAILABLE TO	EMPLOYEES WHOSE EMPLOYER PROVIDES ONE	EMPLOYEES WHOSE EMPLOYER PROVIDES ONE	EVERYONE	EVERYONE WHOSE INCOME IS BELOW $110,000 FOR SINGLE FILERS OR $173,000 FOR JOINT (2012 LIMITS)
INVESTMENT SELECTION	MENU SELECTED BY EMPLOYER	MENU SELECTED BY EMPLOYER	SELF	SELF
ARE CONTRIBUTIONS TAX DEDUCTIBLE?	YES	NO	YES, IF INCOME IS BELOW $58,000 / $92,000 (SINGLE /	NO

			JOINT) OR YOU HAVE NO 401(K) AVAILABLE	
TAX RATE ON WITHDRAWALS	FULL INCOME RATE	NONE	FULL INCOME RATE	NONE
Contribution limit (2012)	**$17,000**	**$17,000**	**$5,000** FOR MOST, **$6,000** IF 50 OR OLDER	**$5,000** FOR MOST, **$6,000** IF 50 OR OLDER
DISTRIBUTIONS	PERMITTED AT AGE 59½; REQUIRED AT AGE 70½	PERMITTED AT AGE 59½; REQUIRED AT AGE 70½	PERMITTED AT AGE 59½; REQUIRED AT AGE 70½	PERMITTED AT AGE 59½; NEVER REQUIRED

TAXABLE (NORMAL) ACCOUNT: USE IT TO SAVE FOR SHORT-TERM GOALS

A plain vanilla taxable investment account lacks any of the tax advantages of a 401(k) or IRA. Investors are responsible for paying taxes on all dividends, interest, and capital gains from the account. Nonetheless, taxable accounts merit a place in just about everyone's portfolio for two reasons:

1. **A taxable account is the right place to save for short-term needs, like a new car, a second home, or a fund for contingencies**. Retirement accounts are poor places to put money that you know you will need before you turn 60, as you may have to pay a significant penalty to access any of your money prior to retirement.

2. **A taxable account is the right place to invest excess savings beyond what can be contributed to a retirement account.** There is no limit to the amount of money that can be saved in a standard investment account.

WHY MOST PEOPLE SHOULD HAVE ALL THREE TYPES OF ACCOUNTS

Because each account type has its own particular advantages, most investors should open and use both an IRA and a taxable investment account in addition to using their company-provided 401(k). It would be foolish not to use a 401(k) that receives an automatic match from an employer, it would be equally foolhardy to pass up on the tax benefits and flexibility of an IRA, and the need for a reserve fund that can be easily accessed at any time makes the vanilla taxable account an essential component of a portfolio.

FURTHER READING

- The financial-services startup Brightscope has a directory of 401(k) plans where you can find your company's offering and see how it ranks compared to other companies in terms of fees, employer matches, participation rate, and account balances.

- The IRS has up to date and very detailed information on the eligibility requirements and contribution limits of the various retirement accounts: IRAs here, Roth IRAs here, SEP plans here.

- If you are curious about when and how you will be required to take distributions from a retirement account, there is also an IRS page on that.

- The IvyVest site discusses tax-loss harvesting, a slightly more advanced technique that can help reduce the taxes you pay in non-retirement accounts.

- Remember to see www.ivyvest.com/book-resources to get links to every article, book, or site discussed in further reading sections.

Chapter 5

Getting Organized:

How to Form Your Own Personal Investing Plan

Overview

Intelligently planning for retirement is much like training for a marathon. Before jumping into investing, it is important to develop a goal for how much you want to have accumulated by the time of your retirement. From this goal, you can determine a yearly savings target and a five-step plan for how much money to invest in each account.

Investing as a Marathon

Running a marathon—a 26.2 mile (40km) road race—is a serious effort that might seem masochistic to most. Yet millions of people are drawn to these races every year, often embarking on months-long training programs that call for them to gradually ramp up the miles they run every week from 20 to 40, 50 miles, or more. One of the things that makes training for and completing a marathon so compelling is that there is a clear and concrete "goal post" at the end of the process. Conversely, the lack of a clearly defined goal post is one of the things that makes retirement planning so frustrating.

The equivalent of the "marathon day" for retirement planning is your expected retirement date. By the time of your retirement, you should have accumulated enough savings to comfortably last you through your senior years. Unlike a marathon, however, retirement has an unknown finish line. Figuring out how much you'll need to live the way you want to is a challenge, but coming up with some kind of goal is essential to designing a "training plan." The exercise in the following section will help.

How Much of a Nest Egg Do You Need?

Estimating the size of the nest egg that you will need to accumulate to live comfortably during retirement involves two major steps. You will have to first assess the amount of income you will need in retirement and then estimate how much of your wealth you will comfortably be able to withdrawal every year.

Estimating the Income You Will Need in Retirement

1. It is useful to consider first the minimum amount of income from your investments you would be comfortable living on in retirement. From this, you can begin to think about the amount of money you will need in your investment accounts at the time of retirement. When thinking about your minimum, or base, annual retirement income target, consider these questions:

    a. How much money are you spending today? This can be a good starting point for what you will spend in retirement.

    b. Do you anticipate having lower expenses in retirement? For instance, will you downsize to a smaller home? Pay off a mortgage? Spend less on children? **Most people can get by on 2/3 of their current income and spending because they will have fewer expenses in retirement.**[9]

    c. Do you or your spouse have a pension plan from a company or the government? Do you anticipate holding a part-time job after retirement? Are you the kind of person that is going to keep working long past 65? Subtract from your figure any additional sources of income you anticipate having in retirement. Consider how much you are projected to receive in Social Security benefits (you can find this on your last Social Security statement).

    d. It is important to note that this does not have to be an exact exercise. Whatever number you come up with, write it down—you will use it in the next step.

2. Next, consider stretch goals and the income needed to meet them. Have you always wanted to travel the world? Buy a yacht? Take a cruise? Just live a more luxurious lifestyle? Write these down and estimate the amount of money you will need to accomplish these dreams in addition to what you will need to cover basic needs. Add this sum to your total from above to get a stretch retirement income target.

ESTIMATING YOUR SAFE WITHDRAWAL RATE

Now that you know what the target income is, the next step is to figure out the total savings you will need at retirement to produce it. In retirement, you will continue to invest your nest egg in the markets so that it continues to grow while you withdrawal some money every year to cover your living expenses. The goal is to have a portfolio that will last 25 years or more after retirement (the typical retirement lifetime).

How much of a portfolio can be safely withdrawn every year is subject to fierce debate, and depends on all kinds of assumptions about inflation, interest rates, and future investment returns. In general, the experts agree that

- If you are very concerned about outliving your assets, have little room to adjust spending in the event of a market downturn, or just want to be extra conservative, a 4% withdrawal rate will protect your assets in all but the very worst bear markets.

- Many people should be able to withdraw 5% of their assets during retirement (this assumes a relatively modest 2% rate of return after inflation over the retirement period).

- If you have significant flexibility to adjust your lifestyle in the event that returns are lower than expected, you might be able to withdraw money at a 6% or 7% rate instead.[10]

To determine the amount of retirement wealth you will need to produce your stretch and base cases, divide the annual target income by the withdrawal rate that's best for you. For instance, if you need $50,000 per year in retirement income (in today's dollars) and have a little flexibility to adjust your lifestyle in the event of a market downturn, then you will need $50,000 / 0.05 = $1,000,000 in savings at the time of retirement. If you require only $20,000 in addition to your other income sources such as social security, and you have great flexibility to adjust your income, then you may need to budget only $20,000 / 0.06 = $330,000 as your end goal. Perform this calculation for both your stretch and base income goals.

DESIGNING A SAVINGS PLAN TO MEET YOUR GOALS

Once they have decided when they are going to run 26.2 miles, aspiring marathoners next have to figure out how to train their bodies to be able to accomplish this feat at the set date. A first step is figuring out a weekly training mileage. Rules of thumb are to build up to a weekly training mileage of about twice the distance of the race (i.e., 40–50 miles a week) and to refrain from increasing mileage in any one week by more than 10%.

The retirement planning equivalent of weekly training mileage is yearly savings. Fortunately, there are some similar rules of thumb to estimate how much you should put into your investments each year in order to meet a retirement goal. We will approach this by calculating what percentage of your final goal you should save each year.

The percentage of your goal that you need to save each year depends on two factors: the returns that you will get on your investments and the number of years you have remaining until retirement. Table 5 shows the relationship of these factors. On the top, are various levels of investment return. On the side axis is the number of years remaining until retirement. The percentages indicate how much of the end goal should be saved each year until retirement.

The kinds of portfolios advocated here have historically been able to achieve returns of greater than 4% a year in real (after-inflation)

terms. Locate the number of years you have remaining until retirement on the left and find the corresponding entry under the "4% return" column. The table also gives you an idea of how the kind of return you expect to get can affect how much you need to save.

TABLE 5 - PERCENTAGE OF END GOAL TO SAVE EACH YEAR PRECEDING RETIREMENT

Years until retirement	3% return	4% return	5% return	6% return	7% return
2	49.3%	49.0%	48.8%	48.5%	48.3%
4	23.9%	23.5%	23.2%	22.9%	22.5%
6	15.5%	15.1%	14.7%	14.3%	14.0%
8	11.2%	10.9%	10.5%	10.1%	9.7%
10	8.7%	8.3%	8.0%	7.6%	7.2%
12	7.0%	6.7%	6.3%	5.9%	5.6%
14	5.9%	5.5%	5.1%	4.8%	4.4%
16	5.0%	4.6%	4.2%	3.9%	3.6%
18	4.3%	3.9%	3.6%	3.2%	2.9%
20	3.7%	3.4%	3.0%	2.7%	2.4%
22	3.3%	2.9%	2.6%	2.3%	2.0%
24	2.9%	2.6%	2.2%	2.0%	1.7%
26	2.6%	2.3%	2.0%	1.7%	1.5%
28	2.3%	2.0%	1.7%	1.5%	1.2%
30	2.1%	1.8%	1.5%	1.3%	1.1%
32	1.9%	1.6%	1.3%	1.1%	0.9%
34	1.7%	1.4%	1.2%	1.0%	0.8%
36	1.6%	1.3%	1.0%	0.8%	0.7%
38	1.4%	1.2%	0.9%	0.7%	0.6%
40	1.3%	1.1%	0.8%	0.6%	0.5%

Multiply the number that you found in the table by your end goal—this is the amount that you need to save on a yearly basis. For example, let's assume you are retiring in 20 years and you need to generate $200,000 in additional savings to meet your conservative goal and $300,000 to meet your stretch goals. Looking at the "4% return" column that corresponds to 20 years, you would find that you need to save 3.4% of your goal every year: 0.034 x $200,000 = $6,800 a year toward the basic goal. For the stretch goal, 0.034 x $300,000 = $10,200 a year.

Finally, compare your annual savings target for your basic goal to your current income and savings rates. Does it seem feasible to save this amount while maintaining your current standard of living, or would it require a difficult lifestyle adjustment for you or your family? Consider the same for your stretch goals. Find a number that is hopefully between your conservative and stretch targets and that still leaves you enough income to live at a comfortable level. This is your annual savings target.

ALLOCATE YEARLY SAVINGS TO DIFFERENT ACCOUNTS THROUGH A SIMPLE 5-STEP PLAN

Once marathon runners have picked a date for their race and decided on weekly training mileage, the final step in their planning process is to split up weekly miles into distinct workouts. The three key workouts in any marathon training program are the long run, the tempo run, and the speed workout.

The retirement plan equivalent is determining how to split yearly savings into different accounts. As with marathon training, there are three choices: the IRA, 401(k), and taxable accounts discussed in the previous chapter. Figuring out how much money to contribute to each is a five-step process.

1. **Contribute enough to a 401(k) to maximize the employer match**. For instance, if your employer matches half of contributions up to 6% of salary, then make sure you are contributing 6% of your salary per pay period. Turning away free money is almost never a

good idea. If you do not have a 401(k) or if your company does not match any of your contributions, skip to Step 2.

2. **Pay off any high-interest debt and build up an emergency reserve in a bank account or taxable account that can cover at least three months of living expenses.** Also consider any short-term goals you might have. It is nice having a buffer in a cash account that can be accessed at any time in case of an unexpected layoff, medical emergency, or other unforeseen consequence. Depending on your degree of risk tolerance, you can choose to build this up over time, or to put all your savings into this fund until it reaches the desired level. Of course, if you have any high-interest credit card debt or anything with an interest rate above 8%, you should pay the entire balance off before you start to build up your cash reserve.

3. **Maximize tax-deductible contributions to an IRA.** If you are eligible for tax deductions on an IRA (or if you are eligible for a Roth IRA), you should contribute any excess savings to an IRA account. Max out your donations every year if you can—the tax benefits and variety of choices in IRA investing are unparalleled. If you exceed the income limit for tax deductibility, skip this step.

4. **Max out tax-deductible 401(k) contributions.** The 2012 limit for tax-deductible contributions is $17,000 per year, which is enough to build up a tax-advantaged war chest. If you don't have a 401(k), skip this step.

5. **Contribute any additional funds to a taxable account.** Though it is last in the process, for investors in high income brackets, the taxable account may grow to become the largest account because of the restrictions placed on the amount that can be invested in retirement accounts.

FURTHER READING

- For a more advanced discussion of how you can use something called Monte Carlo analysis to measure the chance of meeting your goals, see the article on our IvyVest sister site (you can see links for all articles on www.ivyvest.com/book-resources).

- For an academic discussion of sustainable withdrawal rates from a portfolio using various historical simulations, see the "Trinity study." The authors conclude that an investor withdrawing money at a 4% rate and taking a cost-of-living-adjustment every year historically had a 98% chance of a portfolio lasting at least 30 years. With a 5% withdrawal, this probability went down to 83%.

- "Dynamic Retirement Withdrawal Planning," an academic article by two professors at Central Michigan University, discusses the impact of adjustment withdrawal rate in real time on the lifetime of a portfolio. This is the logic for why those with more flexibility to adjust their lifestyles may be able to take more out of a portfolio (at least initially) than those with less flexibility.

- For a more in-depth discussion of various retirement issues, *The Bogleheads' Guide to Retirement Planning* is a good source.

- Purdue University provides ten free online modules on various retirement planning subjects.

CHAPTER 6

WHY YOU NEED TO KNOW YOUR INVESTING ALPHAS AND BETAS:

A GUIDE TO INVESTMENT RETURNS

OVERVIEW

The return of a portfolio investments has two distinct sources. We can think about them as two different kinds of returns. What we will call "beta returns" come from your portfolio's exposure to the overall market. What we will call "alpha returns" come from the difference between your portfolio and the market, which can reflect your skill (or luck) as an investor. Most investors should focus more on beta returns than on alpha returns, as relatively few people in the world are truly capable of producing reliable alpha returns (beating the market). Two financial instruments—ETFs (exchange-traded funds) and index funds—provide reliable and cheap ways to acquire beta returns.

PORTFOLIO MANAGERS AND UMBRELLA SALESMAN

I have always been a believer that you can judge how bustling and entrepreneurial a city is by visiting it in the middle of a rainstorm. In the true entrepreneurial metropolises, you will inevitably find that, shortly after the first raindrops touch the pavement, a smiling man carrying a selection of umbrellas will approach you and humbly offer his wares. I've always appreciated the friendly neighborhood umbrella salesman, and have a collection of rain-protecting devices sitting in my closet as evidence of this (and of my general forgetfulness).

Frequently after such encounters, I've reflected that I would make a terrible umbrella salesman. I fundamentally lack the relentless drive to make a sale that the best umbrella peddlers exhibit. But in the middle of a torrential downpour, even I would succeed. This highlights the rather obvious connection between the success of an individual umbrella salesman and the weather. If you wanted to determine whether an umbrella seller was any good, it would not be enough to examine how sales have been over the past month. You would want to know how the weather affected sales efforts, perhaps by comparing these to the sales of other umbrella sellers in the region.

It turns out that money managers are just as impacted by their environment as umbrella sellers, but the connection seems to be less obvious to many investors, perhaps because market movements are not quite as tangible as raindrops.

THE DIFFERENCE BETWEEN ALPHA AND BETA

Suppose you want to evaluate the performance of your investments. You look at your statements and find out that overall, your portfolio returned 15% last year. This seems good in absolute terms, since the average return of the stock markets since 1900 is around 10% a year.

But knowing that your portfolio returned 15% last year is kind of like saying an umbrella seller sold 5 umbrellas yesterday – it does not really help you unless you put it into context. Was it raining yesterday, or was it sunny? Was the Super Bowl in town? In the context of investing, was last year 1999 (the height of .com mania) or 2008 (the financial crisis)?

To get a better idea of whether that 15% return is good or bad, you could compare it to the return of the overall stock market. If you have a portfolio that is invested in US Stocks, you could use an index like the *S&P 500*.

Suppose you find that the S&P 500 actually went up 20% last year. Now that 15% return does not seem so great in comparison. Your selection of individual investments actually subtracted value. You performed worse than most investors in the market, worse than you should have given the external conditions.

Finance theory formalizes these concepts by splitting the sources of return of a portfolio into two parts: what we will call alpha returns and what we will call beta returns. Formally, beta measures the sensitivity of a portfolio to the overall market and is a generally a function of how risky the portfolio is. Alpha, on the other hand, measures the difference between the return of a portfolio and the return of an equivalent market portfolio (one with an equivalent risk).

The precise details of how to calculate alpha and beta are not terribly important (see the Further Reading section if you are interested). What is important is to understand that any portfolio has two things that affect its returns: the overall market (beta), and the selection of individual investments (alpha).

We will call part of a portfolio's returns that are related to the overall market "beta returns" for shorthand, and the part of a portfolio's returns that are a function of stock-picking "alpha returns" (note this is shorthand and these terms may not appear in other texts). In the umbrella examples, these correspond to weather and salesmanship.

WHY BETA RETURNS ARE POSITIVE (OVER-TIME) AND ALPHA RETURNS ARE NOT

We saw in the first chapter that over very long periods like the last century, the overall stock market has appreciated at about 10% a year, or 6% after accounting for inflation. Since this is a market-level return we are talking about, it is a beta return.

It is worth asking, where does that return come from? In other words, why do stocks have positive returns in excess of inflation over long periods of time?

The answer has to do with the fundamental economic purpose of the stock market – to channel money from individuals that have money to companies that need money in order to build something. If investors were not able to earn a positive return over time, they would refuse to invest. The uncertainty of stock investments means that investors demand to be compensated for the risk that they are taking, which is why stocks should return more than less risky kinds of investments over time.

To put it differently, **if beta returns were not positive over time, there could be no stock market.**

By contrast, **there is no economic reason that alpha returns need to be positive.** Positive alpha returns are the result of luck or skill, not compensation for taking on any kind of risk. This has a very important implication: **alpha is a zero-sum game.** If one investor's portfolio has positive alpha returns (outperformance of the market), there must be at least one other investor out there whose portfolio has negative alpha returns (underperformance of the overall market). Across the universe of all investors, alpha returns must average to zero.

WHY BETA RETURNS TRUMP ALPHA RETURNS

From the above discussion, alpha returns sound quite appealing, since they are the result of skill and not subject to the overall fluctuations of the stock market. Yet there are three strong reasons that most investors should spend the vast majority of their time thinking about beta returns rather than alpha returns.

1. **Beta returns are more important. Statistically, beta is a far more significant driver of returns than alpha.** Study after study has indicated that most of the differences between real-world portfolios are a function of beta. Which particular stocks different portfolio managers own is far less significant than their overall exposure to the ups and downs of the stock market.

2. **Beta returns are much easier to achieve.** Trying to produce positive alpha returns is a losing battle for all but the most elite investors. Studies indicate that 97% of professional mutual fund managers are incapable of reliably beating the market (apart from luck) after deducting their fees. The top 3% may legitimately be capable of producing positive alpha, but they

are hard to find.[11] Buying funds with the best track records is generally not a winning strategy in itself—many of these managers have merely gotten lucky. A few fund managers do seem to produce consistent alpha returns at a high and statistically significant level, but many of the cream of the crop are inaccessible to individual investors, or their funds have gotten too large by the time it is obvious that they have skill.

3.   **Beta returns are much cheaper to achieve.** It is very easy to essentially buy the entire stock market and ensure that you get 100% beta returns by using a low-cost ETF (more on this later). The fees in popular ETFs can be as low as 0.05% of invested assets a year. By contrast, mutual funds that try to select stocks that will outperform the overall market are subject to multiple levels of fees, including a management expense, trading costs, and compensation to the salesperson or advisor that sells the funds. These fees can average 1.3% or more. Fees for hedge funds, which are less-regulated investment vehicles only available to high net worth investors, are even higher. Moreover, there is no certainty that any fund will actually produce positive alpha returns, even before fees are deducted.

YOUR ONE-STOP SHOPS FOR BETA OF ALL KINDS: INDEX FUNDS AND ETFS

Alpha generation is a topic for another book, the remainder of this one will focus on efficient generation of beta returns. There are four ways that investors can purchase diversified portfolios focused on beta returns: active mutual funds, index mutual funds, portfolios of individual stocks, and ETFs.

Mutual funds **are entities that buy a diversified mix of stocks on behalf of their own shareholders.** There have traditionally been many advantages to owning shares in a mutual fund versus owning a diversified portfolio of individual stocks. These include convenience, the ability to split transaction costs over multiple owners, and the benefits of professional management.

Mutual funds come in two varieties: "active" and "passive."

- *Actively managed funds* **try to pick stocks that will do better than the overall market, while still owning diversified portfolios.** Many fund companies hire hundreds of analysts and portfolio managers that meet with company management and do other extensive research on a company's prospects, trying to determine whether the prevailing stock price is too high or low. These kinds of funds attempt to deliver alpha returns and beta returns at the same time. Although they will largely track the market (beta), they may do a percentage point better or worse depending on the skill or luck of the portfolio manager (alpha).

- *Passive funds,* **also called** *index funds,* **are a kind of mutual fund exclusively devoted to delivering beta returns.** Instead of hiring analysts to research which companies to buy, index funds just buy every share in a broad market index such as the S&P 500. Although index funds will not be able to beat the market by definition, this strategy ensures that they will do at least as well as the market (before fees). Because they have no need to hire hundreds of analysts like actively managed funds, index funds are able to charge lower fees.

Exchange-traded funds (ETFs) **are index funds that are traded on an exchange, like stocks.** For investors focused on achieving beta returns, this offers several advantages:

- **Convenience.** Unlike mutual funds, ETFs can be purchased easily through a discount brokerage just like stocks.

- **Tax advantages.** ETFs are less likely than mutual funds to generate taxable gains until you sell the shares.

- **Lower fees.** ETFs often have marginally lower fees than index mutual funds.

ETFs also do have a couple disadvantages relative to mutual funds:

- **Commissions**. Because ETFs are purchased like stocks, you will usually have to pay a small commission to your discount broker every time you trade. However, many brokerages now offer a selection of commission-free ETFs (see below).

- **Liquidity**. Mutual funds are required to redeem shares at their net asset value on a daily basis. With ETFs, there is no such requirement; you are dependent on there being someone else to buy your shares if you want to sell them. However, this is not really an issue except for some small ETFs that might be thinly traded.

Index funds may be a better vehicle for small investors who want to invest a small amount every pay-period or every week (called "dollar-cost averaging") since mutual fund companies like T. Rowe Price or Vanguard do not charge a transaction fee to enter a fund. **However, many discount brokerages have responded by eliminating commission charges on eligible ETFs.** For instance, Vanguard ETFs can be traded commission-free at discount brokerage accounts set up at either Vanguard or at TD Ameritrade.

For those with greater than $50K or so in savings, ETFs may be the most effective way of achieving beta returns, as they combine extremely low fees with the ability to easily buy and sell shares. Those with smaller nest eggs or who expect to be making frequent transactions may want to look at index mutual funds, or at least ensure that they are getting commission-free trades on ETFs.

FURTHER READING

- *A Random Walk Down Wall Street* by Princeton's Burton G. Malkiel is a classic investment text from a famous finance professor that makes a strong case for investing in index funds and ETFs.

- *Common Sense on Mutual Funds,* by Vanguard founder Jack Bogle, discusses the merits of the mutual fund structure in much more detail.

- An academic paper by famous University of Chicago Professor Eugene Fama and Kenneth French makes a longer case about why the data indicate that mutual funds do not add value, and that past "winners" do not continue to outperform in the future.

- A short article on the IvyVest site goes into more detail on mutual funds, ETFs, VC, and other investment options.

Chapter 7

Moving Beyond the Stock Market:

An Introduction to Asset Classes

Overview

By this point, you have consolidated your accounts at one or two providers, opened an IRA (if needed), and set up contributions to your 401(k) and IRA. This chapter will look at the kinds of things that you can actually invest in, including stocks, bonds, real estate (REITs), and commodities.

Sell More Than Just Umbrellas

Despite my genuine praise, I may have been a bit unfair to the enterprising umbrella seller of the previous chapter. The best umbrella sellers are undoubtedly wise enough to realize that their sales are only really going to flourish in one particular type of climate. Unless they live in the Pacific Northwest where it is reliably rainy most of the year, enterprising salespeople will probably balance out their exposure to weather's variability by also selling something people need under other weather conditions, like sunglasses. That way, whether it is sunny or rainy, they can always hawk something.

Similarly, in our discussion of alphas and betas to date we have been a bit unfair in concentrating too much on the stock market, and in particular, the U.S. stock market. It is, after all, possible to put your money in other kinds of investments that may do well at a time when the U.S. stock market does not.

An Introduction to Asset Classes

The analogs of umbrellas and sunglasses in the investment world are the different *asset classes*. Broadly speaking, these are the kinds of "things" that you can put your savings into. They include stocks—which can be further divided into U.S. stocks, international stocks, and emerging markets stocks—bonds, inflation-protected bonds, commodities, and real estate.

STOCKS

Stocks are financial assets that represent fractional ownership in actual companies. Stocks have real value because as companies make money they usually return a portion of the profits to shareholders in the form of cash dividends that are paid every year. In the absence of any kind of stock market, the value of any stock would simply be the expected value of its future stream of dividends, discounted to today's dollars to account for inflation. In the real world where stocks constantly trade hands on an exchange, prices fluctuate wildly because nobody really knows for certain what the value of that dividend stream will be.

Investors in stocks expect to make a return on their investment in two different ways:

1. **Dividends.** The annual or semi-annual payments to shareholders that represent earnings returned to owners.
2. **Capital gains.** Income that arises from when a shareowner sells a stock for a higher price than he or she purchased it for.

Stocks can be split further into different asset classes based on the country where the underlying company resides. The logic of this divide is that the economic cycles of different regions of the world will not always exactly coincide—e.g., Chinese stocks may do well at a time when Brazilian stocks do not.

Domestic stocks are investments in U.S. companies that are usually listed on the New York Stock Exchange or the NASDAQ market. U.S. stocks are the safest investments for U.S. citizens to hold for two reasons:

1. The firmly established legal system in the United States ensures that there is a high probability that the rights of investors will be

protected. This is extremely important since any investment involves giving a certain amount of money away today for an uncertain return in the future. With a less established legal system companies might be tempted to take the money and not give anything back.

2. Since the investments are in companies whose earnings are mostly in dollars, there is less currency risk compared to investing in companies overseas.

International developed-markets stocks are companies domiciled in places like Europe, Australia, and Japan. These are also countries that have long and established histories of capitalism and the rule of law, though the risks for U.S. citizens in investing in other countries may be somewhat greater than in purchasing U.S. assets. The returns to these investments are usually in a different currency like the Euro or Yen. **This creates the risk that U.S. investors will lose money if that currency loses value relative to the dollar.** However, some of these economies may experience higher growth rates than the United States in the coming years.

Emerging-markets stocks from countries like China, India, and Brazil are thought by many to have the highest potential returns as well as the highest potential risks of any stocks. These rapidly developing countries do not always have established histories of capitalism or legal systems, and there is always a small chance that a foreign government will seize foreign shareholders' stakes during the time of a crisis. At the same time, the economies of many emerging-market countries have grown much faster than the U.S. economy in the past decade. It is likely that countries like China and India will, on average, continue to grow faster in the future, because they currently have vastly lower living standards. This does not guarantee that their stock market will outperform the US market, however, since it is possible that the price of their shares already accounts for the expectation of high growth in the future.

BONDS

As discussed previously, bonds are like IOUs to a company or government. Bondholders lend out their money, for a fixed period of time. In return, they are compensated by interest payments at a set period – often every six months. Bonds are considered a safer investment than stocks for a couple reasons:

- With a bond, the borrower makes a promise to pay back the full amount of the loan at the end of the term. With stock investments, there is no such promise.

- In the event that the company is unable to pay back its loans and goes bankrupt (as was the case with Enron and Lehman Brothers), bondholders have the first claim on the company's assets, so they will get paid back in full before stockholders receive anything.

The bond market can be broken into multiple different segments based on the type of entity that is issuing the bond. The major segments include Treasury bonds, corporate bonds, mortgage-backed securities, and municipal bonds.

Investments in federal government bonds (called Treasury bonds because they are issued by the U.S. Treasury Department) **are the safest kind of bond investments because they come with the full backing of the U.S. government,** which has the authority to tax citizens of the largest economy in the world, as well as to print money.

There is also a large market for corporate bonds, which are just bonds issued by corporations in order to fund their capital needs. Because there is always a chance that a company might go bankrupt and not be able to pay back its obligations to bond-holders, these are considered riskier than Treasury bonds, and therefore make higher interest payments to their holders.

Mortgage-backed bonds are, as the name would suggest, bonds that are used to fund mortgages for home purchases. These are often guaranteed by one of the now-famous quasi-governmental agencies, Fannie Mae or Freddie Mac. Because they are implicitly backed by the Federal government, they tend to have interest payments that are lower than corporate bonds. However purchases of mortgage-backed securities are subject to another kind of risk called prepayment risk. In short, since homeowners have the option to refinance or pay their mortgage back early, MBS holders are never quite sure when they will receive their money back (which is not an attractive feature if you are trying to plan for retirement).

Municipal bonds are bonds that are issued by cities and states in order to fund short-term spending needs. "Muni Bonds," as they are known, are primarily interesting because they are tax-free bonds – the federal government does assess normal income taxes on interest payments. This makes them attractive to investors in a high tax bracket who are using a taxable account. However, because of this, muni bonds may sell at a premium to other kinds of bonds, so for investors with a tax-free account or who are in a lower tax bracket, there may be better options.

INFLATION PROTECTED BONDS

Although ordinary Treasury bonds guarantee return of the full amount of the loan, there is no guarantee as to what that money will be able to purchase when it is returned. For instance, imagine "Average Joe" purchases a 30-year Treasury bond with a 5% interest rate for $1,000. Joe will receive $50 every year as well as the return of his original $1,000 after 30 years. However, in those 30 years, the annual rate of inflation (the gradual increase in the price of goods over time) may have also been 5%. Using the "rule of 72" from the first chapter, this means that the price of goods would double about every 15 years (72 / 5 is about 15) and *quadruple* in 30 years. So although Joe did receive his original $1,000 back as planned, it will only purchase him 1/4 of the things that it would have 30 years ago.

Treasury inflation-protected securities (TIPS) were designed to solve this problem for investors. The interest payment that bondholders receive every six months is called a coupon. **TIPS pay a smaller semiannual coupon than normal Treasury bonds, but in return they protect investors from increasing inflation by automatically adjusting both coupon payments and the value of the loan for the effects of inflation.** So in the above example, Joe would have actually received $4,000 back after 30 years, despite only investing $1,000. And he would be able to buy just as many things with his investment as he could have 30 years ago when he made it. In addition, he received his annual interest payments, though they are generally smaller for TIPS than for a regular Treasury bond.

Real Estate (REITs)

Real estate might be the asset class that is the most familiar to the average investor. But many do not realize that in addition to purchasing a personal residence, they can also buy shares in apartments, houses, and commercial holdings like shopping malls. Individuals can invest in real estate through a financial instrument called a Real Estate Investment Trust, but more commonly known by its acronym: REIT. **REITs are legal entities that own properties like apartment buildings, malls, and office buildings.** REITs make money by charging the occupants of their buildings rent every month. They are legally obligated to pass through most of the profits that they make every year directly to shareholders in the REIT in the form of dividends. Because a REIT is a special entity that is required by law to distribute most of its profits every year, it does not have to pay corporate income taxes—a key advantage. REITs are an important asset class to the individual investor, since they often perform well in periods when the stock market is down or when there is high inflation.

Commodities

Commodities are actual, physical resources like oil, gold, and copper. Purchasing commodities outright is distinct from buying the stocks of companies that extract commodities, such as Exxon-Mobil. Investors can own pieces of funds that invest in actual commodities through an innovative new set of ETFs. These funds mimic the process of actually buying and holding physical commodities through the use of what are called futures contracts. It is not absolutely necessary to understand how this works in order to plan for your retirement, but check the further reading section for more details if you are interested. .

Others

Alternative assets like venture capital, hedge funds, and private equity are other options for high wealth and sophisticated investors, but they will not be covered here.

FURTHER READING

- *The Little Book of Common Sense Investing,* by Vanguard chairman John Bogle, is a good place to go if some of the concepts here have not quite sunk in yet.

- For more on the details of stocks, check out the introduction to the topic from the regulatory group FINRA, or see Picking Stocks: A Practical Guide to Investing in the Stock Market, another Ivy Bytes book.

- For more on the mechanics of the bond market, the asset-management group Pimco offers a nice tutorial.

- For more on REITs, see the SEC white paper on the topic

- For more on commodity ETFs see this article on the etfdb.com site for a quick take, or this paper from the Wharton School at U Penn for a much more comprehensive one

CHAPTER 8

WHY THE S&P 500 IS NOT GOOD ENOUGH:

HOW TO USE THE PRINCIPLES OF DIVERSIFICATION TO CHOOSE AN INTELLIGENT ASSET ALLOCATION

OVERVIEW

Choosing your portfolio's overall asset allocation is the most important investment decision you will make. The most important principle to apply in asset allocation is diversification, or investing in multiple asset types. Diversification is the only sure way to increase the expected returns of a portfolio without increasing its risk. To receive the most benefit from diversification, it is not enough to own a large portfolio of stocks or mutual funds. Instead investors must own multiple asset classes such as international stocks, real estate, bonds, and commodities. An intelligent asset allocation plan should resemble ones proposed by the smartest managers of the Ivy League endowments.

COMPLETING THE UMBRELLA ANALOGY

You might be thinking that by this point we have discussed umbrellas more than is warranted in any financial text. Point taken. But thus far one element of our umbrella story is still slightly off. In our hypothetical umbrella market, transactions are between professional salespeople and forgetful ordinary people. But imagine a market composed not of salespeople selling to customers, but of salespeople selling their umbrellas and sunglasses to each other.

What would determine success in a market where everyone was a knowledgeable professional? Hard work, customer service skills, and overall hustle might still add some value. But any success that an individual salesperson had would come at some other salesperson's expense—if someone is charging more than the average price of the items, then someone else is paying more than that price. It's a zero-sum game. The real driver of success would be the choices that each salesperson made when selecting merchandise. A high ratio of umbrellas to sunglasses would lead to success in rainy times, but failure when it is consistently sunny. A salesperson that gambled on sunny weather by stocking up on sunglasses would run into trouble if rain settled in for days.

This is a very close approximation of the situation in the financial markets today. In most stock market transactions, there is a professional on both sides of the trade. It may be possible if you are smart and dedicated and have a lot of time on your hands to produce positive alpha and beat the stock market by picking good stocks. But for most investors, what is really going to matter is what mix of assets classes you purchase. Study after study shows that asset allocation—not stock picking—accounts for the overwhelming majority of differences in the returns of different portfolios.

WHY DIVERSIFICATION IS A FREE LUNCH FOR INVESTORS

On the surface, it might seem that diversification should be a matter of preference. Those with a high risk tolerance might rationally hold undiversified portfolios in the hopes of getting outsized returns, while those that want lower "swings" hold a more diversified portfolio.

This is the case, for instance, in dice. Suppose you are betting on the next number to come up on a single dice. The odds of being right about any one number are 1/6. You could bet on three numbers and you would have a 3 in 6 (50%) chance of being right, but this bet would cost three times as much as a bet on one number, so in the end it does not really matter whether you bet on one number or three. Whether you are diversified or undiversified, if you play the game enough times your returns will be the same.

But investing is different from playing dice. In investing, diversifying actually creates value. **Diversifying your investments allows you to earn greater returns without taking on more risk, or equivalently to take less risk without sacrificing any returns.**

The second of these, how you can reduce the risk of a portfolio with diversification, is pretty clear. Imagine you are given two investments to choose from. Both have an expected annual return of 8%, but both also have a 1 in 5 chance of losing 50% over the next year. If you buy either investment, you will expect to make 8% but have a 20% chance of losing 50%. But what if you buy equal amounts of both investments? Your expected return is still 8%, but now your chance of losing 50% is only 1 in 25 (4%), because it would take both companies having unusually bad years for you to have a worst-case scenario (this assumes the investments are unrelated, that is a bad year for one is not more likely than normal to be a bad year for the other). So your average return is the same, but your risk is smaller. A win-win.

Let's look at another example to see why diversification also can increase returns while keeping risk the same. Suppose that a portfolio invested entirely in stocks runs the risk of losing up to 60% of its value (this approximates the historical peak-to-bottom loss of the market in a really bad market). Not many people are able to withstand a 60% loss. What if you are only able to accept the risk of a 30% loss because of your income needs? One solution is to hold 50% cash and 50% stocks, so your overall portfolio will never fall by more than 30%. Nowadays, however, the return on cash is next to nothing, so you would reduce your total returns by 50% as well. If you expected to earn 8% on average with your all-stock portfolio, you will only earn 4% now.

But if you also have the option to invest in another asset – perhaps called "bonds" – that tends to do *well* in periods when stocks are going to suffer, then your outlook completely changes. Suppose bonds will only return 3% a year on average, but they will return 10% in years in which stocks lose 60%. Now a 50% bonds 50% cash portfolio can be expected to lose 25% in a really bad year, while still making 5.5% on average. But because bonds are diversifying your risk, this actually lets you put even more money into stocks, so you can increase your return even more. Paradoxically, diversifying lets you increase the amount of your money in high-risk assets while accepting the same level of risk as before.

This ability to combine uncorrelated asset classes to smooth returns is extremely important when it comes to asset allocation (more on this in the next chapter). During many periods of recent history, one asset class has done particularly well while another has faltered. For instance, in the 1970s, commodities had a great bull market while stocks performed poorly. In the ugly aftermath of the dot-com bubble, it was real estate that had great performance. And in 2008, Treasury bonds went on a tear when the equity markets were falling apart. So a portfolio of stocks, bonds, real estate, and commodities has lower risk than a portfolio of equities alone, and this lower level of risk, somewhat paradoxically, allows you to keep more money in risky assets that could fall in value, thereby earning greater returns.

This remarkable property is why diversification is a "free lunch." It allows you to avoid the usual tradeoff between risk and return. If you diversify an undiversified portfolio you can get higher returns without increasing the chance of losing money, or you can reduce the chance of losing money without hurting your long-term returns. Nowhere else in finance is this the case. For another explanation of diversification, see this article.

AN S&P INDEX FUND IS NOT A DIVERSIFIED PORTFOLIO

Many have taken the diversification lesson to mean that their portfolio should include as many stocks as possible. One result of this widespread belief is the extreme popularity of index funds and ETFs that track the S&P 500, a diversified market index of 500 of the largest companies in the U.S. These kinds of funds literally hold the stock of every company in the S&P 500.

While index funds and/or ETFs should play an important part in every investor's portfolio, many people have unfortunately drawn the wrong lesson here. **The primary benefits of diversification occur among asset classes and sectors, not among individual stocks**. Once a U.S. stock portfolio includes more than about 25 names, most of the benefits of diversification have already been achieved, because most stocks (particularly those in the same sector) tend to go up and down in sync with one another anyway. Just think of all the stocks you know that went up in 2008—not many.

It is by owning multiple asset classes—foreign stocks, bonds, TIPS, real estate, commodities, etc.—that we can truly consume the "free lunch" of diversification (case in point: TIPS and Treasury bonds had banner years in 2008). Unfortunately, many investors who own index funds have not caught on to this and are not truly diversified, no matter how many stocks their fund owns.

AN INTELLIGENT ASSET ALLOCATION PLAN

A good starting point for creating your asset allocation plan is to look at the allocations of some of the very smartest investors around—the managers of leading Ivy League endowments. Innovative endowments like Harvard and Yale were pioneers in reaching beyond the familiar asset classes of stocks and bonds to add real estate, commodities, international stocks, emerging-markets stocks, and alternative asset classes like hedge funds and private equity. As a result, the Yale endowment has outperformed the U.S. stock market (and the S&P 500) by more than 8% a year over the past 20 years, while also experiencing substantially lower volatility (a measure of risk).

David Swensen, the portfolio manager of Yale University's endowment, recommends this allocation for individual investors:[xii]

- 30% U.S. Stocks

- 20% U.S. real estate

- 15% international developed-markets stocks

- 5% emerging-markets stocks

- 15% TIPS (Treasury Inflation-Protected Securities)

- 15% U.S. Treasury bonds

With a 50% allocation to global stocks, this portfolio has enough "juice" in it to perform well in a time of rising asset prices and high economic growth like the 1990s. At the same time, the 30% allocation to bonds (split between

TIPS and standard Treasury bonds) will hold up well in a bear market like 2008, and the TIPS and sizeable real estate portion will hold up in a severe inflationary environment like the 1970s.

That said, there are a few areas where some investors may want to tweak Swensen's recommendations a bit. (Warning: Esoteric material follows.) Here are some suggestions:

- **Holding a diversified bond allocation rather than U.S. Treasury bonds only.** Swensen recommends holding all bond allocation in the form of U.S. Treasury bonds, or Treasuries, reasoning that corporate bonds do not provide significant diversification to a portfolio that already holds stocks in the same companies. Other gurus advocate holding corporate bonds, mortgage-backed securities, municipal bonds, and international bonds as well, and investors in a higher tax bracket may want to look at municipal bonds.

- **Holding a greater percentage of the portfolio in foreign or international assets.** Swensen's recommendation results in 80% of a portfolio's assets in domestic, U.S. dollar assets. Other finance gurus advocate greater international exposure than this, particularly to emerging markets like China and India.

- **Adding direct commodity exposure.** Swensen's suggested portfolio has a large exposure to real estate, but it does not invest directly in commodities. The ability to easily invest in commodities through ETFs is a relatively new development in the world of finance. Some investors may want to take advantage by adding commodities to their portfolio.

- **Decreasing the allocation to U.S. Treasuries.** Swensen recommends a 30% allocation to U.S. Treasuries, equally split between inflation-protected securities and regular Treasury bonds. Given the current historically low Treasury yields that may be partly a result of unprecedented quantitative easing (or "money printing") from the Federal Reserve, some investors may wish to reduce this allocation.[13]

If you make these adjustments, a large ($200,000 plus), portfolio might include:

- 25% U.S. stocks

- 14% international stocks from developed markets

- 14% international stocks from emerging markets[xiv]

- 15% TIPS

- 7% U.S. Treasuries[xv]

- 9% U.S. real estate

- 7% Foreign real estate

- 9% commodities[xvi]

Some investors may prefer a simplified, "lite" version that includes less tinkering, either because they have a smaller account (under $200,000), or because they just do not wish to mess with so many asset classes. **It is possible to achieve the diversification of the Swensen portfolio by using a single ETF or low-cost index fund that contains three or four asset classes.**

Swensen "lite":

- 50% global stocks

- 15% TIPS

- 20% U.S. real estate

- 15% U.S. Treasury bonds

Unless it is something that interests you, it is not worth getting too bogged down in the details. **The key is to pick a plan that is broadly diversified and makes sense to you, and stick with it.**

SHOULD YOU CHANGE YOUR ASSET ALLOCATION AS YOU GET OLDER?

The conventional wisdom is that you should shift your portfolio into more conservative assets as you approach retirement. One oft-quoted rule of thumb is that the amount of money you should hold in stocks should equal 100 minus your age. So a 60-year-old would only have 40% in stocks (100 – 60 = 40), whereas a 25-year-old would have 75% (100 – 25 = 75). The thinking is that as you get closer to your retirement date, you have less time to make up for any bear markets and are thus less able to take on risk.

This is logical sounding advice, however it is supported by little actual evidence. Historical simulations of how thousands of different asset allocation strategies would have fared over the past century have not shown that decreasing exposure to risky assets at the end of an accumulation period increases the likelihood of a portfolio's success at all (here "success" was defined as a portfolio that outlived its owner).

If you have built up a bit of a war chest that you do not want to risk in the markets, an alternative to adjusting the asset allocation of your investment portfolio is simply to increase the size of your emergency reserve fund. For instance, let's say you are lucky enough to have $5 million and you decide that you want to ensure that $1 million is as risk-free as possible. To protect the $1 million, you put it into bank accounts or short-term TIPS and then invest the remaining $4 million.

A LITTLE HELP?

Have something to say about what you are reading so far? Is something confusing? Tell me about it, and as a small thank you, I will send you a free guide to the essential questions to ask before purchasing any stock. I know from experience that the material in this short checklist can save you thousands of dollars.

If you are reading on a tablet device, click here to take a two-minute survey. Otherwise, point your web browser to http://www.ivybytes.com/feedback.

Feedback will remain totally anonymous and will be used to improve this book for future editions.

FURTHER READING

- Our IvyVest sister site has an excellent free tutorial on asset allocation that is a great accompaniment to this chapter.
- *Unconventional Success: A Fundamental Approach to Personal Investment,* by David Swensen, head of the famous Yale endowment, talks in much more detail about optimal asset allocation for the individual investor, among other topics.
- *Pioneering Portfolio Management* by the same author, discusses the strategies that Yale's endowment took to deliver market-beating performance.
- The U.K.'s Open University provides a free online course on investment risk that might be of interest to those who want to understand this important concept better.

Chapter 9

Putting It Into Practice: How to Painlessly Implement Your Target Asset Allocation Using ETFs

Overview

Once you have determined your desired asset allocation, actually achieving it is pretty easy. There are ETFs you can use to get directly own individual asset classes. Two key factors to consider when picking individual ETFs are cost and liquidity. A short list of good ETFs from Vanguard and iShares will get just about any investor to his or her goal. ETFs can be purchased from a discount brokerage just like common stocks. Implementing investments in a 401(k) can be more complicated, because employers may limit your investment options. When deciding which investments to house in tax-sheltered accounts, it is important to remember a few rules.

How to Achieve a Target Asset Allocation in Five Minutes or Less

Once an asset allocation has been selected for a portfolio, it is easy to find an ETF that provides one-stop buy-it-and-forget-it exposure to that asset class. A list of ETFs by asset class can be found at http://etfdb.com/etfdb-categories or in the table below.

When you must choose between multiple funds that offer exposure to the same asset class, consider these two important factors:

1. **Fees.** Expenses for ETFs should be well under 0.5% of assets (often referred to as 50 "basis points," where 1 basis point = 0.01%)—the lower the fee the better.
2. **Liquidity.** *Liquidity* is a measure of how active the market is for a stock or ETF. If the market for an ETF is not very active, there

might be a large gap between the buying and selling price. This gap, called a "spread" is an implicit transaction cost that you must pay every time you buy or sell an ETF. Look for larger ETFs (in terms of assets under management) to avoid a high spread.

A STARTING POINT: GOOD ETFS FOR EACH ASSET CLASS

The following is a list of well-run ETFs that have relatively low management fees and good liquidity. The *ticker* is the three or four letter "code" given to all stocks and ETFs—you will need it when it comes time to enter your orders at your discount brokerage. Vanguard offers excellent index mutual-fund equivalents for those that prefer investing in that structure.

Table 6 — ETFs to use for a one-stop portfolio (all figures as of February 2013)

Asset class	Suggested weight	Ticker	Expense Ratio
U.S. stocks	25%	VTI	.05%
International stocks (developed markets)	14%	VEA	.12%
Emerging Markets stocks	14%	VWO	.18%
U.S. real estate	9%	VNQ	.10%
Foreign real estate	7%	VNQI	.32%
TIPS	15%	TIP	.20%

US Treasuries	7%	TLT	.15%
Commodities	9%	DBC	.87%
Global stocks[a]	-	VT	.19%
U.S. total bond market[b]	-	BND	.10%
Gold[c]	-	GLD	.40%

[a]VT can replace VTI, VEA, VEO and get entire stock allocation with one ETF if you desire a simpler approach.

[b]BND can replace TLT. Some gurus like David Swensen believe that it is not worth adding corporate bonds if you already own stocks – others disagree.

[c]Gold can be used in place of some or all commodities exposure, or pulled from TIPs (e.g., 12% TIPs, 6% gold, 6% commodities would work).

HOW TO PURCHASE ETFS

ETFs can be purchased through a discount brokerage exactly like stocks. Simply select the "Buy/Sell" or "Trade" option from the brokerage home page, enter the stock ticker of the ETF you want to purchase, and enter the number of shares you wish to buy. The ETFs in the table above are fairly liquid, so it is safe to use a *market order*. This means that your order is immediately fulfilled at the prevailing price on the stock exchange. The alternative is to use a *limit order* in which you manually set the price at which you want to buy or sell shares. Limit orders are fulfilled when one person is offering to buy at the same price another is offering to sell.

To determine the number of shares of each ETF to buy, follow these steps:

1. **Multiply the dollar value of your total portfolio by the allocation to the asset class.** This will give you the total dollar value of your investment in the ETF. For instance, if you desire a 20% exposure to U.S. stocks and you have a $100,000 total portfolio, you would want to buy $20,000 of Vanguard's total stock market ETF to achieve this.

2. **Divide the dollar value of your desired ETF investment by the share price of the ETF and round down to the nearest share.** If you wanted to invest $20,000 in Vanguard's total stock market ETF and it was trading at $10 a share then you would want to buy 2,000 shares.

DEALING WITH THE 401(K)

ETFs are cheap and easy to buy in any discount brokerage account. But if you are investing in an employer sponsored 401(k) retirement plan (and you *should be* if one is available to you) then you may only have a limited set of mutual funds to select from. This limitation is one of the reasons many investors choose to rollover their 401(k) to an IRA as soon as they leave a job.

However, very good choices may be available to you inside of a 401(k), it may just take more work to separate the good from the bad. Although the mutual fund industry as a whole habitually fails to add any alpha (and charges a lot anyway), there are fund families that offer you a decent shot of getting good value for your fees. There are three strategies for dealing with your 401(k):

1. **Buy an equity index fund for U.S. or international stocks.** At a minimum, most plans should offer a U.S. equity index fund, which you can use for your U.S. equity allocation. If possible, look for one labeled "Total Stock Market" or "Extended Stock Market." This fund will include smaller companies that are typically left out of the more common S&P 500 index. You may also use an "International

Equity Fund." Look to see whether this is based off of the *EAFÉ Index* (an index created by Morgan Stanley that serves as a benchmark of the performance of developed equity markets in regions like Europe, Australia, and Southeast Asia). If it is, you can count this as your international developed-markets exposure.

2. **Find a good actively managed equity fund.** Picking an actively managed fund can be trickier than picking an index fund, so only try it if you are willing to spend a little time with research. It is important that you purchase a diversified fund that will primarily deliver beta returns, so look for broad funds that would fall in one of the categories defined above, like emerging-markets, U.S., or international developed-markets stocks. Avoid sector or theme-focused funds, as they will provide inadequate diversification. The Morningstar website is a great place to find information about actively managed mutual funds. Look for one with these characteristics:

    a. **A reasonable expense ratio (should be less than 1% of assets).** Mutual fund fees are quoted as a percentage of your overall investment, and known as a management expense ratio. Low expense ratios are one of the only factors that academic studies have consistently associated with positive future performance.

    b. **Low (under 60%) share turnover.** Morningstar publishes a "turnover" figure that indicates the percentage of a fund's portfolio that is turned over (bought and then sold) every year. Academic studies show that mutual funds that trade frequently are likely to underperform their peers. Frequent trading carries significant explicit and implicit costs that can negatively affect a fund's performance. Find a manager that is willing to take a more long-term view, with a turnover of 60% or less.

    c. **A good long-term track record.** The Morningstar rating is a good proxy for past performance, since it measures the fund against its peers. Although past performance is unfortunately not terribly predictive of future performance, there is some evidence at least that bad funds can remain consistently bad. Ratings go from one to five stars—try to find a fund with at least a three-star rating, but don't get carried away searching for five stars.

d. **A portfolio manager with a long tenure**. One of the problems with mutual funds is the high rate of manager turnover. Great past performance might not mean that much if a different manager conducted the orchestra. Try to find a fund with a manager that has been around for at least four or five years.

3. **Buy a bond fund**. If you cannot find a good actively managed fund that falls into one of your asset class categories and you still have more money to allocate, use your 401(k) for the bond piece of your portfolio. These are also good funds to hold in a retirement account, since you will be protecting yourself from paying taxes on the high income they generate (more on this next). If your plan offers a Real Estate or REIT fund, this is also a good choice.

What to Put in Which Account

If you have a taxable account as well as one or more retirement accounts, then you will have to decide which asset classes to hold where. It is important to take the most advantage of the tax savings offered by retirement accounts by using them to hold assets that will generate the most amounts of taxable income. Practically, this means the following:

- **REITs and taxable bonds should be kept in retirement accounts as much as possible.** REITs and bonds both pay large dividends or interest payments every year. If they are not held in a tax-free account, these payments will be taxed at the ordinary income rate.

- **It is okay to hold long-term stock ETFs in a taxable account.** Since ETFs are highly tax-efficient instruments that rarely distribute taxable capital gains, they are good candidates for a taxable account. Of course, dividends will still be subject to taxation, but many of them will be at a lower 15% qualified dividend rate. Capital gains from selling ETFs will also be taxed at the lower 15% rate.

- **TIPS should be held in a retirement account.** There's a special tax rule that requires you to pay taxes on certain income that has not even been received yet. (When your bond principal is adjusted for inflation, this increase is considered income, even though you do not see the money until the bond matures.)

FURTHER READING

- Our IvyVest sister site has an excellent free tutorial on asset allocation that is a great accompaniment to the past two chapters (was mentioned last chapter too, but it applies here as well).
- Vanguard's ETF page is worth checking out for information on the funds that they offer, as well as another overview of what ETFs are and how they work
- If you want a more detailed view of how ETFs are created and managed from an institutional view, check out the howstuffworks.com tutorial

CHAPTER 10

MAKING IT BULLETPROOF:

HOW TO MANAGE FOR THE LONG-TERM WITH A LOCKBOX (AND A SANDBOX)

OVERVIEW

Many individual investors achieve poor investment returns because they trade too much, often purchasing investments that have appreciated in value and selling those that have depreciated. "Buy high, sell low" is not a good investment strategy. A better approach is to put your investment strategy on autopilot by consciously not changing your asset allocation or investment mix unless there is a significant change in your own circumstances. But you can keep the majority of savings in your "lockbox," while devoting a much smaller pot of money to "playing around" in the market.

THE INVESTING WISDOM OF *SATURDAY NIGHT LIVE*

One of the all-time great *Saturday Night Live* skits came from the 2000 presidential campaign. A very funny Darrell Hammond lampooned Al Gore for saying "lockbox" every other word during the 2000 presidential debates. The root of the humor was that Gore wanted to keep the entire Social Security surplus segregated from the rest of the yearly government budget items. He did not want Congress to be able to "fiddle" with this money by using it to fund more tax cuts or spending programs. Although Gore's insistence on a lockbox provided plenty of comedic value at the time, subsequent years have shown that a lockbox may have had real value, as Congress quickly turned a budget surplus into an enormous deficit.

Similarly, it is important for the individual investor to keep the vast majority of his or her savings invested in a long-term buy-and-hold allocation that will not change with the times, as everyone can be tempted by the little voice telling us to go for some flashy, but stupid, investment. Have faith in your allocation plan. The benefits of long-term investing, and the perils of frequent trading, have been proven without a doubt.

WHY YOU SHOULD KEEP MOST OF YOUR ASSETS IN YOUR LOCKBOX

Like the one that Al Gore wanted to create for the Social Security surplus, a lockbox is a place where investment returns can pile up without interference from their owner. **With a lockbox you make a plan and stick to it, regardless of what is going on in the stock market.**

A lockbox is a great approach for these reasons:

- **Using a lockbox prevents you from making the worst mistake that plagues most investors—letting emotion dictate investment strategy.** As a whole, we have seen that individual equity investors significantly underperform the market. A major reason for this poor performance is the human tendency to look around at the crowd and buy what everyone else is buying and sell what everyone else is getting rid of. In other words, we buy assets that have recently appreciated and sell those that have recently depreciated. Thus, people rushed to get their money into technology stocks in 2000 at the peak of the dot.com bubble and rushed out in 2002 at the low. The same story played out with real estate stocks a few years later. By keeping a lockbox, you will be immune to this "buy high sell low" destructive tendency, and thus automatically outperform the average investor.

- **Using a lockbox keeps you from overtrading**. People who trade frequently think they can outsmart the stock market. But even most professional investors and traders don't outperform the market average. The majority of professionally managed mutual funds underperform the stock market averages every year. Without taking time to do huge amounts of research, there is little reason to think that you will be any more successful with your own trades. Instead you will likely rack up commission costs and increase your chances of relying on your emotions and making a costly mistake.

- **Using a lockbox minimizes the transaction costs that eat away at the returns generated by active strategies.** Every time you buy or sell a stock, you rack up trading costs. You can minimize these costs by trading infrequently.

Creating a lockbox is relatively simple. **Choose your asset allocation, pick good assets, and keep your account on autopilot going forward.** Ignore the talking heads on CNBC and refrain from changing your strategy or investment mix unless at designated times and for very good reasons.

Here is how to build your personal lockbox:

1. **Create a target asset allocation plan** and change it infrequently (perhaps never).

2. **Implement your plan** with either index funds or ETFs. Choose one fund (or absolutely no more than two) for each asset class in your plan.

3. **Rebalance your portfolio** to return it to your target asset allocation at a set schedule of once or twice every year. No changes should be made outside of that schedule. Rebalancing is important because some asset classes will grow faster than others over time, and thus come to dominate a larger portion of your portfolio's assets.

WHY YOU SHOULD ALSO KEEP A (SMALL) SANDBOX

Some investors (author included) may have cringed just a bit at the idea of an immutable lockbox. A lockbox clearly makes sense, but it's a little boring. If you want investing to be fun and dream about the thrill of owning a 10-bagger stock (don't worry if you don't know what that means), by all means take a shot. **But do so with only 5% to 15% of your savings in a "sandbox."** The sandbox is where you can have some responsible fun, make "bets" on individual stocks or sectors, and truly manage your own money.

In addition to being a bit more exciting than the "buy it and forget it" plan, the sandbox serves two extremely important functions:

1. **It is educational**. A sandbox provides a reason to learn a lot more about investing. If you think that IBM might be a great buy right now, you are probably going to want to know how to value the company, whether it looks cheap or expensive on various metrics, how management is doing running the company, etc. Looking for answers to questions like these can be a hugely educational process that will make you into a more confident and informed investor better able to stick to a plan. You might find that you hate thinking about investing, and that is fine. Nothing is stopping you from investing your sandbox in ETFs or mutual funds, or closing it altogether. But you also might turn out to be one of those 2–3% of investors who are capable of consistently beating the market, and it would be a shame to let those talents go to waste.

2. **It provides a release valve for our impulse to trade more often than is healthy**. As mentioned earlier, one of the reasons for a lockbox is investors' checkered history with the market. "Follow the herd" thinking has caused many to run headlong into technology stocks, commodities, housing, or even tulips (search for Dutch tulip mania), at the exact wrong time. But the lockbox is only going to be as strong as the will of the investor that created it. And there will come a time, no matter how strong the will, that every individual investor will see other people getting rich and want to jump into the fray, or will see his or her wealth disappearing and just want to sell everything. The sandbox lets you make a compromise with yourself—if you *really* think that "pets.com" is going to be the next Walmart, then by all means, put a little of your sandbox account into it, but don't endanger your retirement by investing all of your assets in it.

BEST PRACTICES FOR SANDBOX DESIGN

Introducing a sandbox does add some complexity to the fairly straightforward process for determining which investments to hold in each account that has been described thus far. Following these principles will help you manage your sandbox account:

- **Open a different account for the sandbox to keep it segregated from your lockbox**. The sandbox does not have to be a separate account per se, but it may be easier to segregate it from the lockbox by opening up a separate account to house it. For instance, if you use a Vanguard account for your other money, consider opening an E*TRADE account for your sandbox.

- **Consider using an IRA for your sandbox**. Because you may be buying and selling investments a few times a year in your sandbox, it is likely that you will generate taxable capital gains from time to time. This makes the sandbox a good candidate for a self-directed IRA.

- **Maintain discipline about the size of the sandbox**. Do not let it creep above 20% of your assets.

Let's say an investor wants to put 15% of assets in a sandbox and has $200,000 in retirement savings split across several accounts, with $50,000 in a 401(k), $100,000 in traditional IRAs, and $50,000 in a taxable account. This investor might split the accounts between the lockbox and sandbox as shown in Table 7.

TABLE 7 — A TYPICAL ARRANGEMENT OF A PORTFOLIO USING THE LOCKBOX AND SANDBOX MODEL

Lockbox	Sandbox
401(k) with T. Rowe Price $50,000	IRA with E*TRADE self-directed $30,000 (15% of total)
IRA with Fidelity contains bond and real estate ETFs $70,000	
taxable brokerage account with	

Fidelity contains stock ETFs $50,000	

CAVEATS

A few caveats:

- If you have less than $100,000 in assets, it may make sense to build up your lockbox before you open up a sandbox.

- Be careful not to trade too much, even in your sandbox. Even small commissions can eat up a nest egg if you are trading more than a few times a month.

- Unless you have a huge amount of time and skill, day trading is almost always a losing cause (see the paper by Barber and Odean listed directly below in Further Reading).

FURTHER READING

- The sister IvyVest site has a free tutorial on portfolio management which discusses different rebalancing techniques and also introduces tax-loss harvesting, a legal means of reducing taxes in a taxable account.

- For more on the psychological considerations of investing and why a lockbox is a good idea, see the very comprehensive SEC research on the topic, or read the slightly more summarized IvyVest tutorial on behavioral finance.

- For more on how trading is hazardous to your wealth, read the seminal paper on the topic, by professors Brad Barber and Terrance Odean of the University of California.

CONCLUSION AND SUMMARY

My hope is that you have come away from this book with

- An understanding that investing does not have to be as complicated as it is sometimes portrayed, and that making it more complicated often actually *decreases* your returns.

- An appreciation of some of the ways that you can make investing more complex if you want to, and some idea of where to go to find out more about it if you are interested.

- (Most importantly) the confidence to seize control of your own financial future.

The intent of this book was to accomplish these three things in as readable and concise of a way as possible, while still not oversimplifying things. I hope this came across through ten chapters, each of which dealt with a particular facet of the retirement planning or investing process.

Chapter 1 the story of Jill and Average Joe, made it clear that this investing stuff really matters. Because of compound interest, seemingly small differences in when you start investing, and in how you invest, can make huge differences in the amount of money you have at retirement. These considerations are not merely an academic matter—Jill ended up with a retirement income five times greater than Joe solely because she started saving 10 years earlier and didn't make a few key mistakes.

Chapter 2 took a step back and introduced the concepts of stocks, bonds, and intrinsic value. Purchasing a stock is like becoming a partial owner of a company, buying a bond is like becoming a lender to a company. The intrinsic value of any investment is the cash it will produce in the future, discounted to the present to reflect the time value of money. This is an important point often neglected: Investments only have a fundamental value to the extent that they pay us money in the future.

Armed with this background, Chapter 3 jumped into the practical: how to choose an investment account. Mutual fund accounts, discount brokerage accounts, full-service brokerage accounts, and bank accounts have advantages and disadvantages for the investor. Discount brokerage accounts are compelling choices for investors willing to manage their own money, since they have rock-bottom expenses and unparalleled access to just about any investment under the sun.

Chapter 4 explored how to use retirement accounts like a 401(k) and IRA to save money in taxes. Everyone who is eligible should take advantage of the tax breaks retirement accounts offer, as the benefits can compound over time (a frequent theme of this book) to reach surprising levels. To properly take advantage of these completely legal and ethical breaks, you should have a taxable investment account for short-term and overflow savings, a 401(k) (if your company offers one), at least one IRA, and a bank account.

Chapter 5 discussed a topic that, lamentably, many investors often overlook: how to form a retirement savings and investing plan. Using a simple exercise, you make a ballpark estimate of how much money you should be saving to reach your retirement goal. Then you allocate that money every year to different accounts. First, take advantage of any 401(k) employer matches, next deposit sufficient savings in your emergency reserve fund, then contribute the maximum you can to your IRA and 401(k), and finally put money into a taxable account.

Chapter 6 introduced the concepts of alpha and beta as the two sources of an investment's returns. Alpha measures the difference between a portfolio or stock's return and that of the market, and is a result of skill (or luck) in selecting securities. Beta measures an investment's sensitivity to the market, which will have a positive return over time because investors need to be compensated in order to keep taking risks. Although alpha seems attractive if you can get it, beta is the dominant source of most real portfolios' returns. Alpha returns sum to zero across the overall market, making pursuing it a losing goal for most investors.

Chapter 7 looked at the different asset classes you can invest in, including stocks from the United States, Europe, Japan, and emerging markets, both normal Treasury bonds and TIPs (inflation-protected bonds), Real Estate Investment Trusts, and commodities.

Diversification, one of the most important principles in all of investing, was explored in Chapter 8. There is more to investing than just buying a diversified portfolio of U.S. stocks. Diversification can reduce risk without reducing returns, or equivalently it can increase returns without reducing risk. If you want to create your own diversified asset allocation plan, look at the mix the managers of the Ivy League endowments use. A model portfolio like the one recommended by David Swensen, manager of the Yale endowment, is a great place to start.

Chapter 9 examined how to actually implement that allocation plan using exchange traded funds (ETFs). ETFs are a great (relatively) new financial instrument that acts like a combination of a stock and a mutual fund and provides a low-cost, tax-efficient way to get broad exposure to the markets. I suggested specific ETFs that you can use to implement each asset class in your portfolio.

Chapter 10 looked at how to manage your portfolio on an ongoing basis. Because different asset classes will perform differently over time, it is periodically necessarily to rebalance your portfolio by buying or selling assets to restore their weight to the target you designated. It is essential to think of the lion's share of your savings as being in a lockbox that you should not touch (other than to rebalance). If you want to play around in the market you can create a sandbox account, in which you place a much smaller percentage of your portfolio.

If you have found this book helpful, please consider recommending it to a friend or family member. The epidemic of financial illiteracy that costs individual investors billions of dollars every year can only be tackled one mind at a time!

Either way, thanks for reading, and please keep in touch with us at www.ivyvest.com (investing) and www.ivybytes.com (publishing).

BONUS OFFER

GET A FREE COPY OF *THE DEFINITIVE CHECKLIST OF QUESTIONS TO ASK BEFORE PURCHASING ANY STOCK*

I hope that you have found this book an efficient way to get beyond the headlines and sound bites and learn more about a topic critical to everyone's future.

I would love to get your feedback. Let me know what you think of this book by completing a one-minute reader survey by clicking this in-text link or pointing your web browser to www.ivybytes.com/feedback. As a small thank you, I will send you the Ivy Bytes white paper on the essential questions you must answer before you buy any stock. I firmly believe that printing this checklist and going through it before you buy any investment can save you *a lot* of money.

If you did enjoy the guide, please also consider writing a review on Amazon. Your reviews will be greatly appreciated and will help other readers find this book.

You may also be interested in Picking Stocks: A Practical Guide to Investing in the Stock Market, which goes into the process of investing in common stocks much more than this text. And either way, you should definitely check out www.ivyvest.com, which is an extension of this book that contains a lot more free investing resources and tools.

Either way, we would love to keep in touch with you!

- Follow us on Twitter at www.twitter.com/ivybytes

- Find us on Facebook at www.facebook.com/ivybytes

- Check us out on the web at www.ivybytes.com

- Email us at feedback@ivybytes.com

OTHER IVY BYTES BOOKS ON FINANCE

Picking Stocks: A Practical Guide to Investing in the Stock Market

GLOSSARY

401(K) – A retirement plan that is provided by your employer but for which you bear the responsibility of contributing to and managing. Usually, you have a choice from a menu of mutual-funds chosen by your employer.

Actively Managed Fund (or Actively Managed Mutual Fund): An investment fund (usually a mutual fund) that hires a manager and/or research analysts to pick stocks that are expected to perform better than the overall market based on research. Most active funds, however, fail to deliver on this after accounting for the additional fees that they charge.

Alpha: A measure of the difference between the return of a portfolio and an equivalently risky investment in the overall stock market. Positive alpha is a result of skill (or luck) in selecting individual stocks or investments.

Beta: A measure of a portfolio's sensitivity to the overall stock market. A beta of '1' indicates that, on average, the portfolio will go up 1% when the overall market goes up 1%.

Bid-Ask spread: Financial markets function somewhat like continuous auctions, where buyers enter orders to purchase securities for a set price that are known as "bids" and sellers enter orders to sell securities at a given price that are known as "asks." When a buyer and seller agree on the price, an order is executed. The bid-ask spread is the difference between the highest bid and the lowest ask for any share. For instance, if the highest bid for a stock is $32.50 and the lowest ask is $32.58 then the bid-ask spread is 8 cents. The bid-ask spread is a measure of the implicit transaction cost that someone that buys and then sells a stock using market orders would pay.

Bond: A bond is a type of an investment that most closely resembles a loan. An entity like a corporation or government can issue and sell a bond that makes a fixed payment (known as a coupon) at set periods over the term of the loan. At the end of the loan, the amount is returned in full. Bonds are financial securities that can be traded like stocks.

Commodities: Physical and tangible assets like copper, iron-ore, wheat, corn, and gold. Individual investors can acquire exposure to commodities through a variety of ETFs which either directly own and store the raw materials, or "virtually" own them by using futures contracts.

Coupon: The amount that a bond pays every period (most commonly, every six months).

Deflation: The opposite of inflation, deflation occurs when price levels fall over time, such that $1 will buy more in the future than it does today. Deflation occurs rarely at the level of the overall economy, as inflation is much more common. However deflation can occur in the aftermath of a financial crisis (and has been prevalent in Japan for much of the past 15 years).

Discount Broker or Discount Brokerage: A trading firm, frequently operating online, that will take custody of your money and execute trades at your discretion, usually for a low flat-fee per trade. Discount brokers differ from full-service brokerages and financial advisors in that they do not offer much in the way of financial advice. Popular discount brokers include ETrade, Fidelity (which is also a mutual fund company), TD Ameritrade, and Scottrade.

Dividend: The periodic and variable payment that a company may make to its shareholders, usually representing a return of some of the profits of the company to its legal owners.

Emerging-Markets Stocks (also "developing markets"): Stocks in companies that are based in countries whose economies have lower average incomes than the United States and might not yet be totally modernized, but are generally growing faster than the US. Examples include: China, India, Brazil, South Africa, Russia.

Equity Investment – An investment in a stock or the stock market. Given this name because in buying a stock you are becoming a fractional owner ("getting equity") of a company.

Exchanged-Traded Fund (ETF): An ETF trades in real-time on an exchange like a stock, but offers ownership in a diversified portfolio of stocks in one shot, like an index mutual fund. ETFs have a mechanism that allows them to increase or decrease the number of shares in existence, and also keep the share price in the market very close to their net asset value.

Expense Ratio (or Management Expense Ratio) – The fees that a mutual fund charges per year, expressed as a percentage of the total assets that you have invested in the fund (e.g. 1%).

Index (also "Market Index"): An average created to track the performance of an overall market. Usually reflects every stock in a country or sector, weighted by the size of the company. Examples for the US include the Dow Jones Average and the S&P 500.

Index Fund (Also "Passive Fund"): A mutual fund or ETF that tries to "match" a market index by buying and holding substantially every stock in the index. Unlike actively managed funds, index funds do not attempt to do research to pick stocks that will out-perform the market. Consequently, their fees tend to be much lower than actively-managed funds.

Inflation: The increase in the cost of living over time, measured in percentage increase per year. With high inflation, we will have to pay more for the very same goods in the future. Inflation has averaged 2-3% per year over the long-term (with significant volatility around this over the short-term).

IRA (Individual Retirement Account) – A retirement account created by the Federal government that allows workers to put away money for their retirement tax-free. Contributions to an IRA are tax-deductible (up to a fairly small limit) in the year of the contribution, and earnings and dividends accrue tax-free until withdrawal.

Limit Order: An order for a stock or ETF placed through a broker that is to be executed only if the price hits the level set. Buy limit orders are known as a "bid," since you are offering to purchase the shares for a given price. Sell limit orders are known as an "ask". A buy limit order for a stock at $32.50

will execute only at $32.50 or less. If nobody is willing to sell the shares at that level and the stock trades higher, the order may never execute.

Liquidity: A measure of how active of a market there is for a particular security or type of security. Liquid markets contain many different buyers and sellers, which makes for tight bid-ask spreads, and means that it is easy to get into or out of a position. Illiquid markets feature infrequent transactions and relatively few buyers and sellers.

Market Order: An order for a stock or ETF placed through a broker that is to be executed immediately at the prevailing price in the market for that security. If the market order is a buy order, the order will be executed immediately at the price of the lowest 'ask' to the person willing to sell shares for the lowest price. If the purchase is a sell order, the order will be executed immediately at the highest 'bid.' See also bid-ask spread.

Municipal Bond: A bond issued by a US city, state, or other municipality. "Muni bonds", as they are often known, have the key characteristic that interest on them is exempt from Federal taxes. Normally, interest from bonds is taxed at the ordinary income rate.

Mutual Fund: A mutual fund is an investment fund that purchases multiple stocks on behalf of its own shareholders. Mutual funds enable individuals to cheaply and efficiently acquire diversified portfolios of stocks, which would be difficult and expensive to do on their own. When you purchase a mutual fund, you are purchasing a share of its total investment portfolio. Any gains or dividends on that portfolio will be distributed to you annually. Mutual funds are not traded on an exchange like stocks or ETFs; they are purchased directly through mutual fund companies like T. Rowe Price, or indirectly through a financial advisor or broker.

Passive Fund: See Index Fund.

Present Value: The approximate worth, in today's dollars, of a future income stream. Reflects the fact that money in the future will not be worth as much as money today due to inflation.

Real Estate Investment Trust (REIT): A type of company that purchases and then rents out real estate like commercial office buildings or apartment buildings. In exchange for paying out substantially all of their profits every year to their shareholders as dividends, REITS are not required to pay taxes at the corporate level. Offer investors exposure to the real estate asset-class.

Registered Investment Advisor (RIA): An investment-advisor who is regulated by the SEC (or the state) and has a *fiduciary duty* to act in the best interests of his or her clients at all times. Distinct from "investment consultants" or full-service brokers who do not have such a duty.

Roth IRA: A special kind of IRA where contributions are not tax deductible, but withdrawals are tax free. A Roth IRA may be favorable if you believe your tax rate will be higher in retirement than it is today, when you are contributing to it.

TIPS (Treasury Inflation Protected Securities): Bonds issued and backed by the US Government that are indexed to inflation. As the cost of living goes up over time, the coupon payments and ultimate value of the bond will go up as well.

Secondary Markets: A market where stocks or bonds are traded in real-time, similar to a continuous auction. Examples include the New York Stock Exchange and the NASDAQ market. Called "secondary" because shares are usually traded from one person to another person, with the company that issued them not taking any part.

Treasury Bond: A bond issued and backed by the US Government, thought to be low risk since it is supported by future tax revenues (as well as the Federal Reserve's printing press...).

Notes

---

[1] Figures are computed in present, inflation-adjusted dollars based on 6% real returns for Jill (rate of the overall stock market) and 2% for Average Joe (inferred rate of the average investor in equities, see below data from DALBAR, a respected financial research company). If anything, the difference between Jill and Average Joe given here may be understated, as recent DALBAR data show equity investors earning real returns of about 1% over this period.

[2] This assumes Jill has a retirement lifetime of 20 years, continues to earn an average investment of 10% a year in retirement, and draws her portfolio down to a zero balance at the end of 20 years. Actual withdrawals may be lower than this in the earlier years if Jill wanted to be prudent. To minimize the chances of running out of money, some financial planners recommend a maximum withdrawal rate of 4.5%.

[3] The U.S. stock market had a compound annual growth rate (CAGR) of 9.5% in nominal (not adjusted for inflation) terms and 6.33% in real terms from 1900 through the end of 2010, according to the helpful calculator at http://www.moneychimp.com/features/market_cagr.htm.

[4] According to DALBAR's 2011 Quantitative Analysis of Investor Behavior (QAIB) report, which examined investment returns over the past 20 years, equity investors received 3.83% annual compound returns versus 9.14% for the S&P 500, a broad U.S. market index. See http://www.qaib.com/public/about.aspx.

[5] The exact number is difficult to compute, but domestic mutual funds had a 0.78% average fee in 2010 according to the Morningstar report, http://news.morningstar.com/articlenet/article.aspx?id=378492 (requires a free sign up to read). Registered investment advisors charged an average of 0.9% according to the study quoted in *Investment News,* http://www.investmentnews.com/article/20090922/FREE/909229985.
Investors also paid an unknown but significant amount in commissions and loads to advisors, brokerages, and salespeople.

[6] Data from the 2011 Investment Company Institute Fact Book, Google Finance.

[7] SEE "NOT SO FAST: THE RISKS POSED BY HIGH-FREQUENCY TRADING," BUTTONWOOD COLUMN, AUGUST 6, 2011, PRINT EDITION. AVAILABLE ONLINE AT HTTP://WWW.ECONOMIST.COM/NODE/21525456.

[8] See http://en.wikipedia.org/wiki/Keynesian_beauty_contest for a brief explanation of Keynes's theory.

[9] Empirical evidence of this ratio comes from the U.S. Consumer Expenditure Survey, conducted by the Bureau of Labor Statistics. This survey reports spending between 58% and 66% of pre-retirement income. See http://www.bogleheads.org/wiki/Surveys_of_retirement_spending for a helpful analysis.

[10]   See http://www.fpanet.org/journal/CurrentIssue/TableofContents/SafeSavingsR ates/ for a discussion of the withdrawal rates that would have been possible historically.

[11] See E. F. Fama and K. R. French, "Luck versus Skill in the Cross-Section of Mutual Fund Returns," *Journal of Finance,* 65 (2010): 1915–47.

[12] From *Unconventional Success: A Fundamental Approach to Personal Investment* by David Swensen (Free Press, 2005).

[13] Artificially low Treasury bond yield may arise from two sources. The U.S. Federal Reserve purchases Treasury bonds as part of its normal open market operations to manage the short-term interest rate (currently set at 0), and as a part of any quantitative easing programs. Foreign central banks purchase Treasuries to maintain their currencies at levels below those that might exist in a free market.

[14] This may seem to be an aggressive allocation to emerging markets to some, however it may be conservative relative to the economic footprint of

the emerging world. In the August 2011 article "Power Shift," the *Economist* reported that emerging economies now account for more than 50% of world GDP at purchasing power parity and almost 40% at market exchange rates.

[15] Bond allocation could be modified to include a broader mix of securities by including international bonds, and/or corporate bonds and mortgages. We chose the narrower Swensen suggestion of Treasuries only here because this piece of the portfolio is primarily intended to provide some protection in the event of a prolonged deflationary depression, a scenario in which corporate bonds and mortgages could suffer. Additionally, we would rather get international exposure through real estate and stocks, which arguably have less chance of default or expropriation.

[16] It is also somewhat controversial to include commodities in a portfolio. However they provide clear diversification benefits, inflation protection, and, since they are globally traded, partial protection against a collapse in the value of the U.S. dollar. Readers with an appropriate bent may want to substitute physical gold for part of a commodities allocation. If desired, it may make sense to pull from TIPS for half of this.

[17]   See http://www.investmentnews.com/article/20121002/BLOG09/121009987   by Rob Arnott